T0328702

Cambridge Elements ≡

Elements in Second Language Acquisition
edited by
Alessandro G. Benati
University College Dublin
John W. Schwieter
Wilfrid Laurier University, Ontario

INPUT

John Truscott
National Tsing Hua University

CAMBRIDGE
UNIVERSITY PRESS

Shaftesbury Road, Cambridge CB2 8EA, United Kingdom

One Liberty Plaza, 20th Floor, New York, NY 10006, USA

477 Williamstown Road, Port Melbourne, VIC 3207, Australia

314–321, 3rd Floor, Plot 3, Splendor Forum, Jasola District Centre, New Delhi – 110025, India

103 Penang Road, #05–06/07, Visioncrest Commercial, Singapore 238467

Cambridge University Press is part of Cambridge University Press & Assessment, a department of the University of Cambridge.

We share the University's mission to contribute to society through the pursuit of education, learning and research at the highest international levels of excellence.

www.cambridge.org
Information on this title: www.cambridge.org/9781009500890

DOI: 10.1017/9781009063609

First published 2024

A catalogue record for this publication is available from the British Library.

ISBN 978-1-009-50089-0 Hardback
ISBN 978-1-009-06531-3 Paperback
ISSN 2517-7974 (online)
ISSN 2517-7966 (print)

Cambridge University Press & Assessment has no responsibility for the persistence or accuracy of URLs for external or third-party internet websites referred to in this publication and does not guarantee that any content on such websites is, or will remain, accurate or appropriate.

Input

Elements in Second Language Acquisition

DOI: 10.1017/9781009063609
First published online: June 2024

John Truscott
National Tsing Hua University
Author for correspondence: John Truscott, truscott@mx.nthu.edu.tw

Abstract: Input is the name of a topic – the way that language "out there" impacts the development of interlanguage, within the individual. It is perhaps the most important aspect of second language learning. This Element offers an overview of the key concepts related to input and the major lines of research exploring its nature and its role in second language learning. It then puts things together into a coherent, if controversial, picture of input and its role in development, emphasizing the place of consciousness. In this and most other current perspectives, implicit (unconscious) input-based learning is the heart of second language acquisition. This suggests two general options for teaching: (a) trust the natural implicit processes, trying to create optimal conditions for them; (b) direct those processes to selected features of the input, probably using explicit instruction. The conclusion is that (a) appears preferable.

Keywords: input, second language acquisition, perception, language teaching, language learning

ISBNs: 9781009500890 (HB), 9781009065313 (PB), 9781009063609 (OC)
ISSNs: 2517-7974 (online), 2517-7966 (print)

Contents

1 What Are the Key Concepts?

Success in learning a second language depends, naturally, on exposure to the language. We need very extensive experience, and we need to "take in" what we experience. But the human mind is not a recording device, passively absorbing whatever it encounters. It is, rather, a complex information processor, using its own principles and knowledge to make sense of the things "out there" – things like instances of language – and adjusting its knowledge accordingly. Thus, a central topic in second language acquisition (SLA), and perhaps *the* central topic, is how the human mind deals with the language around us. It is the topic of **input**.

As a major research area, this topic is naturally rich in terminology. In presenting this terminology, I will begin with some terms that are not directly about input but are always present in the background and so deserve some consideration. This is followed by an extended discussion of "input" itself, after which I will consider more specific concepts related to input, some from the study of the mind and others primarily related to teaching.

1.1 Some Background Terms

A key background term that is typically *left* in the background is **language**. It can be defined in many different ways, from many different perspectives. Perhaps the most important dividing line falls between cognitive and social/cultural perspectives. Language can be seen as something in an individual's head or it can be seen as a feature of social relations and the cultures within which they are embedded. It is undeniably both and therefore can be and must be studied from both perspectives, with the ultimate goal of establishing a unified explanation.

The concept of input belongs primarily to the cognitive side of this divide.[1] Cognitive theory owes a great deal to the computer metaphor, seeing the mind as an information processor. It receives information through the senses, processes and stores the information, retrieves that information when needed, and uses it to produce output in the form of actions, including speech. In this metaphor, input is the information taken in by the computer, or perhaps the process of taking it in. The nature of this "taking-in" process represents the fundamental issue for the study of input.

From a cognitive perspective, looking at what is inside our heads, language is the interaction among a number of distinct types of knowledge and ability. These types include, at least, **phonological** (linguistic sounds), **morphological**

---

[1] Note, for example, the very skeptical attitude expressed by Lantolf, Poehner, and Thorne (2020) toward the concept.

(the structure of words), **syntactic** (the ways that phrases and sentences are constructed), **semantic** (the meanings of linguistic units), **pragmatic** (meaning in social context), **articulatory** (the muscle movements that produce speech), and **orthographic** (written forms). This *non-monolithic* character of language will assume some importance in Section 4.

A *second* language shares this character, as it also includes sounds, structured sentences, meanings, and physical control of speech. The cognitive conception of a second language is well captured in the term **interlanguage** (Selinker, 1972). It refers to the knowledge of L2 learners, which is to say the state of their underlying linguistic system at any given point. The term has the advantage of being theory neutral, its main claim being simply that there *is* a system, not just scraps of information or modifications of the first language. To the extent that a given learner can use the language fluently and competently, the interlanguage is what makes this use possible.

The nature of the system has always been a source of dispute, and ideas have shifted over the years (see Tarone, 2014, for a useful summary). Contrary to Selinker's (1972) original conception, interlanguage has generally come to be seen as a genuine language. Partly for this reason, universal grammar (UG) theorists (see 2.6) have embraced the concept, as it fits well with their overall conception of second language and second language learning and provides a useful way to frame major issues. The dynamic nature of the system has also come to the fore, though the details are again a theoretical issue. One important aspect is variability – not just over time, but also from one context or task to another. Research, from various perspectives, has also been dedicated to the discovery of more or less predictable ways in which interlanguage develops, on its own terms, not simply reflecting the character of the L1 or the target language. The L1 was originally given a prominent position. This role was subsequently challenged, but now it is once more recognized as a significant factor, though theoretical divergence occurs on exactly how it affects the interlanguage. Not withstanding the many disagreements, the idea of interlanguage as a developing system has become a key part of SLA and is likely to remain so.

If the interlanguage is a system, what about language-related knowledge that is not an integral part of that system? Such knowledge clearly does exist. An English learner who has been taught a given grammar rule might never manage to incorporate that rule in the interlanguage or use it in speech or writing but still be aware of it and be able to talk about it. A Mandarin learner who has little or no ability to produce the tones of the language or hear them in speech might still know that the language has four tones and be able to accurately describe them. Linguistics students may have mastered concepts like the Theta Criterion or feature interpretability, but it is unlikely that this knowledge will ever become part of their interlanguage for any second language they are learning.

This language-related knowledge has been referred to with a variety of terms, with somewhat varying meanings, notably including **metalinguistic knowledge, knowledge *about* language** (as opposed to knowledge *of* language), **learned knowledge** (as opposed to *acquired* knowledge), and **Learned Linguistic Knowledge** (as opposed to *competence*). It has also been associated with the notions of explicit knowledge and declarative knowledge, though considerable caution is required here. I will refer to it herein as "metalinguistic."

1.2 Input

Many definitions have been offered for the term "input." It is commonly understood in a traditional, intuitive way, partly reflecting the computer metaphor, and this makes a good starting point. But researchers have been aware for some time that considerable complexity lurks behind this neat metaphor. To understand input, we need to get beyond the surface, considering how it fits into the cognitive system as a whole.

1.2.1 Input: Basic Conceptions

Intuitively, the meaning of "input" seems clear. When we hear someone speak in the language that we are learning, what they say is input. When we read something in the language, what we read is input. Input is then "the material that is used for acquisition." It is no surprise that the term **evidence** commonly appears in this context. Input is taken to be the evidence that learners use to determine the underlying nature of the language. The learner is then a kind of detective, or problem-solver, figuring out the principles of the language on the basis of available information – which is embodied in the input. In this conceptualization, input/evidence is naturally seen as instances of the language, providing information about its characteristics. The input-as-evidence idea can be seen in the term **primary linguistic data** commonly used in UG approaches, to be described in Section 2.

We normally think of input as what the learner gets from other people, but learners also hear (or read) the things that they themselves say (write), so input is sometimes taken to include their own production. This has been called **virtual input** (Sharwood Smith, 1981), **auto-input** (Schmidt & Frota, 1986), and **backdoor learning** (Terrell, 1991). We can imagine it playing a meaningful role in second language learning, and anecdotal evidence exists that it does play such a role, but to my knowledge the question has not been seriously investigated.

1.2.2 Complications in the Basic Conceptions

It is disturbingly easy to think of input as simply the language that learners are exposed to. But things are much more complex than such a surface view would suggest. First, we know that not everything learners hear actually contributes to their learning. For this reason, Corder (1967) introduced the notion of **intake**, to distinguish what is available for learning (input) from what actually gets used (intake). This distinction has become a standard part of thinking in the field, and it is the first step in developing a more sophisticated conception of input.

Krashen (1981, 1982) emphasized that in order for input to be useful (to become intake, in Corder's terms) the learner must be able to understand it, to derive its meaning. If I listen to a speech given in Swahili, I will not be acquiring Swahili. The practical point is that learners need materials that are not *too* difficult for them. The term **comprehensible input** has thus become a standard part of the vocabulary in the field. Mason and Krashen (2020a) characterized **optimal input** as that which is not only comprehensible but also abundant, rich in language, and "compelling" (see also Krashen, 1982). Krashen's (1985) **Input Hypothesis** holds that comprehending input (optimal or not) is the essence of language acquisition.

It is important to recognize that the comprehension can come from a variety of sources, including the learner's existing knowledge of the language but also such things as context, background knowledge, visual clues, translation, or direct explanation. This extra support can turn "too difficult" into "comprehensible," allowing learners to take advantage of input that goes beyond their current knowledge of the language. Another kind of support is **foreigner talk**, the ways that native speakers of a language adjust their speech to make it more comprehensible to a non-proficient speaker. It commonly includes slowing down, speaking more loudly, simplifying, repeating, and pausing.

The concern with intake and comprehensibility brings out the importance of looking not just at what the learner is exposed to, but also at what happens to it as a result of the exposure. This point is reflected in Sharwood Smith's (1993) definition of input as "*potentially processible* language data which are made available, by chance or by design, to the language learner" (p. 167, emphasis added). If a learner is not capable of doing anything (consciously or unconsciously) with an instance of the language, it is not input. An alternative would be to say that it is input of an irrelevant sort, what Corder would classify as input that will not become intake. The important point is that a study of input, however it is defined, must focus on language processing.

This insight has been expressed in a variety of ways. Gass (1997), for one, proposed that two stages precede the intake stage. **Apperception** connects the input to existing knowledge (or its absence) and can thereby identify an aspect of the input as significant, setting it up for further processing. This is followed by the stage of *comprehended* input, which then leads to the intake stage, at which the new information is incorporated in the grammar. Carroll (1999) argued that a series of distinct stages of analysis lies between the immediate sensory experience and the language learning mechanisms, each step in the construction process producing the input for the following step. For MacWhinney (2001), key to understanding acquisition is the way that learners use the various available **cues** in processing their input, cues such as word order, morphological markers, word meaning, and animacy.

Many researchers have stressed the importance of problems or limitations in learners' processing of their input. VanPatten's (2020) **Input Processing** is based on the observation that learners need to process their input correctly in order to benefit from it; training and practice in appropriate processing, focusing on places where things are likely to go wrong, thus becomes a worthy avenue of research. Pienemann's (2020) **Processability Theory** holds that input is only useful if the current developmental state of the processor allows the learner to successfully process it. O'Grady (2015) and Clahsen and Felser (2006) also stress, each in their own theory, the importance of difficulties and limitations L2 learners face in processing input. For N. Ellis (see N. Ellis & Wulff, 2020), the essential problem in L2 learning, distinguishing it from L1 learning, is that L1 processing experience has essentially set the system to ignore some aspects of the L2 (**learned attention, blocking**), so these aspects are in effect removed from the learners' input.

The bottom line, again, is that we cannot understand input just as something out there. We also need to look at what goes on inside the learner's head. What is out there retains an important role in any discussion of input, but also crucial are the learner's ultimate interpretation of it and the process by which this interpretation is derived. It is perhaps best, then, to think of input not as a particular "thing" but rather as the name of a general topic: How what is out there comes to affect what is in the learner's head.

1.3 Key Concepts Taken from Psychology

The importance of input for SLA lies in the contribution it makes to learning, and so **learning** can also be considered a key term in this area. Learning has always been a central concern of psychology, with ideas about it changing considerably over the years. A good contemporary account comes from Dehaene (2020), who defines learning like this: "to learn is to form an internal model of the external world" (p. 5). He stresses that this model building is based on innate constraints – "Learning … always starts from a set of a priori hypotheses, which are projected onto the incoming data" (p. 26). Learning a language means forming a number of such models for the different components of language, based on innate constraints. The "incoming data" can be called input.

In SLA, the term "learning" is often used quite broadly, to mean simply positive changes in memory or ability. In this sense it is interchangeable with its companion term, **acquisition**, though a distinction is sometimes drawn between the two. Krashen in particular distinguished between a natural, unconscious process of acquisition and a more limited, conscious process of learning. When the process is viewed as natural and spontaneous development, the term **growth** is sometimes favored. The most neutral term is **development**.

L2 theory has conceptualized learning in a variety of ways. In UG approaches, for example, it means setting innate parameters, a process that is based on innate principles as well as existing settings (possibly the L1 settings) and of course input. Traditional skill-based approaches see learning as explicit study followed by proceduralization of knowledge and automatization of the resulting rules. In usage-based approaches, the heart of learning is statistical tallying of items in the input. Regardless of approach, a distinction is commonly drawn between **implicit** (unconscious) and **explicit** (conscious) learning. Increasingly important as well is the distinction between **declarative** and **procedural learning**, which is often seen now as a preferred alternative to dividing learning into implicit and explicit types (see Section 4).

The term **incidental learning** is sometimes associated with implicit learning but is probably better seen as the *absence of an intention* to learn (Schmidt, 1990). If a learner is only concerned with getting the meaning from input but in the process becomes aware of some aspect of form, learning that results from this encounter would be incidental but explicit, not implicit.

Memory can be thought of simply as what is learned, perhaps as the internal models of the world referred to in Dehaene's definition of learning. And this simple view is often good enough for practical purposes. A serious interest in theory introduces a great many complications. Maybe for this reason, psychologists' presentations of memory often do not include a general definition of the term, only of individual types of memory (e.g., Baddeley, Eysenck, & Anderson, 2020). Alternatively, they offer lengthy discussion of complications inherent in the concept (e.g., Tulving, 2000).

One important complication is that memory comes in a number of varieties. The most widely accepted categorization scheme starts by distinguishing **long-term** (LTM) from **short-term memory** (STM). Long-term consists of **procedural memory**, which is the knowledge underlying skills of all sorts, and

declarative memory, which is then split into memories of events (**episodic memory**) and memory of facts (**semantic memory**). In SLA, the term **knowledge** typically covers the things that might otherwise be called long-term memory, as seen in the common terms **implicit/explicit knowledge, procedural/declarative knowledge** and, more generally, knowledge of language.

To these can be added **working memory**, a variant on the traditional idea of short-term memory emphasizing its active nature – we hold things in STM in order to use them. Increasingly important in SLA research is variation among learners in their **working memory capacity**, particularly how such variation correlates with success in various aspects of learning.

In current conceptions (see Baddeley, Hitch, & Allen, 2021; D'Esposito & Postle, 2015), working memory can almost be equated with **attention** – the things we are paying attention to are "in" working memory. The concept of attention has a long and very rich history in cognitive and neural research (see Cohen, 2014; Nobre & Mesulam, 2014), especially in the context of perception, and so, not surprisingly, has received extensive application in SLA. The logic of the application is straightforward: We are most likely to remember something, and to remember it most clearly and strongly, if we pay attention to it, so we might expect learners' attention to input and to given aspects of it to be important for language learning. Attention has been closely associated with consciousness, in the cognitive literature and in SLA, though it would be a mistake to equate the two (Koch & Tsuchiya, 2012). Serious study of attention, like serious study of memory, takes us beyond the intuitive notion that we normally assume and introduces some complexities, to which I will return later.

Another important concept is **consciousness** (or **awareness**, often used as essentially synonymous). The term has been used in many different ways in different areas, but the meaning that is relevant here is the experiential one: We are conscious when we are in a normal waking state and unconscious when we are asleep or in a coma; we are conscious *of* something when that something is part of our immediate experience. The role of consciousness, in this sense, has always been a key issue in second language learning, if often implicitly. To what extent is learning a conscious process? Differing answers have inspired (or perhaps justified) differing approaches to teaching.

A number of common terms are related to consciousness. Krashen's (1981, 1982) conscious **learning** and unconscious **acquisition** are foundational concepts in the field, though the use of the terms has faded. The preferred terms now are **explicit** (conscious) and **implicit** (unconscious), reflecting prominent work in cognitive psychology (see Reber & Allen, 2022). The terms distinguish both two types of learning and two types of knowledge. Especially important in the context of input are Schmidt's (1990) notions of **noticing** and **noticing the gap**

(Schmidt & Frota, 1986). Noticing, for Schmidt, referred to a conscious registration of something present in the input, without regard to whether the learner knows what that something is or what it means. The term is commonly used with a much broader, ordinary language meaning, though. Noticing the gap is awareness that something in the input is not consistent with the current state of the interlanguage, though again the term is often used loosely. Prominent in the literature is Schmidt's (1990) **Noticing Hypothesis,** which states that awareness of features of the input – "noticing" – is necessary for their acquisition.

Perception, the way that information from the senses is processed and interpreted, has not received a great deal of explicit attention in SLA. But input processing is itself a form of perception and so the concept deserves recognition here. I will consider it in some detail in Section 4 (for introductions to perception, see Mather, 2011; Wolfe et al., 2018).

Other significant concepts in the area of input involve its emotional, or **affective,** aspect. It is generally agreed that language learning and language use are influenced by emotions such as anxiety, pride, and embarrassment, as is expected given the nature of perception, learning, and memory in general. Krashen (1981, 1982; Dulay, Burt, & Krashen, 1982) captured the relation in his **affective filter,** the idea being that negative emotion prevents input from reaching its destination, that is from being used in acquisition. Sharwood Smith (1996) briefly considered a possible positive role of affect, suggesting that in order to be useful for learning, input requires an affective "validation." In the Modular Cognition Framework (Truscott & Sharwood Smith, 2019) this led to the notion of **value** assigned to instances of input and therefore to the target language and aspects of it (see Section 4). Dulay, Burt, and Krashen's (1982) **speaker models** and Beebe's (1985) notion of **learner preferences** also address the relation between affect and input. The idea, in each case, is that learners attend specifically to the speech of people that they choose as their models and not to that of others, in effect selecting the input that they want to take in.

1.4 Key Concepts Associated with Instruction

A number of relevant terms are associated primarily with language instruction. One group involves the increasingly popular approach of using the target language, wholly or in part, to teach content. Such instruction is not intended specifically to provide extensive input, but this feature tends to dominate, if only because the classroom setting is more conducive to listening experience than to speaking experience. This type of instruction includes **immersion, content and language integrated learning, bilingual education, content-based instruction, content-based language teaching, dual language education,** and

English medium instruction. The ideas and practices overlap greatly, a single type is commonly divided into several sub-types, and the terms themselves can have different meanings to different people (see, for example, Cenon, Genesee, & Gorter, 2014). The details of this confusing picture are peripheral to a discussion of input and so I will not pursue them here.

Instruction often includes efforts to provide learners with as much input as possible, spawning a number of common terms. **Extensive reading** is what its name suggests. Variant terms, sometimes involving limited adjustments, include **free voluntary reading, sustained silent reading, guided self-selected reading**, and **pleasure reading**, the latter term bringing out the emphasis commonly placed by proponents on the importance of learners' enjoyment. **Narrow reading** focuses on works dealing with a particular topic or by a particular author. Paralleling extensive and narrow reading are **extensive listening** and **narrow listening**. To these can be added **extensive viewing**, which takes advantage of the visual clues provided by videos, for example. Its natural companion term is **narrow viewing**.

Long (1983) argued that input is most effective when it occurs in the context of **interaction**. On this idea, instruction should emphasize two-way communication, in which **negotiation** between the participants results in modification of "the interactional structure of conversation." Intimately associated with interaction is **focus on form**, introduced by Long (1991). He defined it in part by contrast with **focus on forms**. The latter is essentially traditional grammar instruction, especially that following a grammatical syllabus. In focus on form, in contrast, activities are meaning-focused but with aspects of form explicitly addressed in the context of those activities. This can be seen especially now in **task-based instruction**. Input is a natural part of such instruction and the interventions are likely to be focused on aspects of the input, but it is only one part of the instruction.

Discussion of this topic requires some caution because "focus on form" has not always been used with the meaning that Long gave it. After Long's proposal, the term became very popular, to the extent that it was sometimes applied to instruction and research that looked more like focus on form*s*. That said, the idea has generated a tremendous amount of research and will no doubt continue to do so. The looser term **form focus** is also in common use.

Intimately associated with interaction, as well as focus on form, is **corrective feedback**. It is a prominent research topic in both written and oral contexts. Particularly noteworthy in this context are **recasts**, which might well be considered a form of input.

Student: I yesterday went to the library.
Teacher: You went to the library yesterday.

Finally, ideas about **output** have acquired a prominent place in SLA, notably in Swain's (1985, 2005) **Output Hypothesis,** which holds that comprehensible input must be supplemented by output practice.

Sharwood Smith (1981) introduced the idea of **consciousness raising**, in which learners discover features of the language guided by the teacher in different ways and to different degrees. To avoid the implication that changes in the learner's state of mind (consciousness) are an essential feature of the process, he later offered **input enhancement** as an alternative term (Sharwood Smith, 1993), highlighting the fact that it is an external adjustment, which might or might not be reflected in the learner's mind. This term has since become an institution in the field. As it is usually understood, input enhancement is about making selected aspects of input more salient in the hope that this will facilitate acquisition of those aspects (see Sharwood Smith, 1991, 1993).[2] A teacher or textbook writer might place past tense endings in bold, for example, to draw learners' attention to those forms. The oral equivalent would be to stress the forms.

An alternative to making a feature especially salient in a given instance is to provide input that contains many instances of that feature. A text might be written to include repeated use of passive forms, for example. This idea of an **input flood** (Trahey & White, 1993) was included in early notions of consciousness raising (Rutherford & Sharwood Smith, 1985), though it was only noted briefly and without the name. It might be considered a form of input enhancement, and is sometimes used in combination with more prototypical varieties.

The notion of **salience** is crucial here, and also has more general significance for SLA. Learners' success in acquiring a linguistic element might be affected by whether that element is especially salient or especially nonsalient in the input. The term has most often been used in an intuitive sense, making serious study difficult, but efforts have been made to deal with it in a more solid and scientific manner (see Gass, Spinner, & Behney, 2018).

2 What Are the Main Branches of Research?

Because input is tied up in one way or another with almost everything in SLA, identifying branches of research on input is challenging, and decisions are to some extent arbitrary, especially because extensive overlap exists among various branches, as they deal with intertwined issues, though often in different terms. I will focus on research that is most clearly, explicitly about input but will sometimes wander away a bit as needed.

---

[2] Sharwood Smith originally had a broader meaning in mind, but this *perceptual* interpretation of input enhancement, one major part of the original idea, has become the standard interpretation.

2.1 Maximizing General Exposure to (Comprehensible) Input

If input, and comprehension of input, is the heart of learning, then a natural goal for instruction is to maximize the learners' exposure to the language, in ways that facilitate comprehension. Some approaches to teaching adopt this as their primary goal (Asher, 2012; Krashen & Terrell, 1988; Mason & Krashen, 2020b; Winitz, 1981, 2020). Not surprisingly, a significant amount of relevant research exists.

2.1.1 Extensive Reading and Its Variants

Extensive reading has been extensively researched. A noteworthy example is the book flood approach of Elley (1991, 2000). Elementary school learners were presented with a large number of books, selected to be of interest to them. Class activities included reading aloud by the teacher, discussion, and sometimes writing, so this was not "pure" extensive reading. The goal was, however, to provide learners with extensive exposure to the target language with a focus on meaning rather than form. The approach was used in a number of countries, focusing on the South Pacific but extending beyond this region. In each case Elley reported strongly positive results, using a variety of tests.

A number of reviews and meta-analyses of extensive reading research are available (Day et al., 2016; Jeon & Day, 2016; Nakanishi, 2014, 2015; Ng, Renandya, & Chong, 2019). The research has addressed a variety of possible benefits, including vocabulary learning, reading comprehension, reading speed, writing, and grammar – with generally positive findings. Thus, the case for extensive reading is quite strong, though most would see it as one important part of an overall program rather than a method in itself (see for example the interview with Paul Nation – Iswanda & Paradita, 2019).

An interesting variant of extensive reading, again, is narrow reading (Krashen, 2004), focusing on works on a particular topic or by a particular author. This approach serves the basic goals of improving comprehensibility and enhancing pleasure (assuming learners are allowed to choose their topics), as well as recycling vocabulary to make it more easily remembered. Research is limited but offers some reason to think that it is beneficial for vocabulary learning (Chang, 2019; Cho, Ahn, & Krashen, 2005; Kang, 2015).

Extensive reading might or might not be supplemented in various ways. Additions are typically used to assist or check comprehension, as in the use of glosses and comprehension questions, though a variety of exercises can and have been used as well. When grammar is the focus of the activities, we are leaving the realm of "maximizing general exposure" and moving into focus on form (see discussion). The boundary between the two is, however, somewhat fuzzy, because grammar and meaning are of course intertwined with one another. When a teacher points to the word *women* to clarify that more than one woman is involved or to *was* to tell learners that a passage is about something that was true in the past, this does not mean abandoning a meaning-focused approach. But it is, in a limited way, bringing in a form focus, drawing learners' attention to form. It thus belongs to an inevitable gray area between simple meaning-oriented exposure and form focus.

2.1.2 Extensive Listening and Viewing

The logic of extensive reading is naturally applied to extensive listening (see Ivone & Renandya, 2019), and the two are sometimes combined. Research is much more limited than that on extensive reading, and there does not seem to be any systematic effort to empirically evaluate its effectiveness, particularly in relation to the much more established practice of intensive listening. The limited research focuses instead on issues of how it should be carried out (see Masrai, 2019; Matsuo, 2015; Rodgers, 2016; and sources cited by them). The effectiveness of the Story-Listening approach has been examined in several studies, with favorable results reported (Mason & Krashen, 2020b; Mason, Smith, & Krashen, 2020). Narrow listening (Krashen, 1996), paralleling narrow reading, has also received some limited investigation. Tsang (2022) and Chang (2019) found it beneficial for spoken proficiency and vocabulary learning, respectively.

TV, movies, videos, and lectures are a natural source of aural input, contributing visual information that can assist comprehension, so extensive viewing is an additional, and possibly improved, form of extensive listening (see Webb, 2015), along with its natural companion, narrow viewing (Rodgers & Webb, 2011). The line between extensive and non-extensive is far from clear, and so discussion of the former can readily lead into a vast literature on incidental learning, especially vocabulary learning, through various media, often supported by a variety of aids for comprehension and/or explicit learning, again leading into the realm of form focus. I will not try to deal with this literature here.

2.2 Input Enhancement and Input Flood

Input enhancement, again, is about making selected aspects of input more salient in the hope that this will facilitate acquisition of those aspects. The idea of enhancing input has generated a considerable amount of research (for review, see Benati, 2016; Gascoigne, 2006; Han, Park, & Combs, 2008; Lee & Huang, 2008; Nassaji, 2017; Pellicer-Sánchez & Boers, 2019). Results have been inconsistent and not particularly impressive overall. Inconsistent results are commonly attributed, at least to a large extent, to differing methodologies, with unclear implications. Making sense of the findings probably also requires us to place them within a broader understanding of the mind, which is to say within a general theoretical framework (Sharwood Smith & Truscott, 2014a). If we want to understand how adjustments in learners' input impact their learning, we first need a clearer idea of how input is processed. Another limitation of the research is that the focus is almost always on the strictly linguistic aspects of the input. The focus could be expanded to include enhancement of other aspects, such as affect and context.

The alternative to standard input enhancement is to provide input that contains many instances of a selected feature, like simple past tense forms – an input flood. This approach has received much less attention in the research, but a number of studies have been done, a typical conclusion being that the flood can, inconsistently, help learners produce correct instances of the language but does not help them avoid incorrect instances (for review of the research, see Benati, 2016; Nassaji, 2017; Pellicer-Sánchez & Boers, 2019).

2.3 Noticing and Noticing the Gap

The terms "noticing" and "noticing the gap," ubiquitous in the literature, embody the idea that consciousness has a central role in second language learning. Paradoxically, their origin lies in Krashen's (1983) discussion of the way that input is used, *un*consciously, in acquisition. He suggested that learners "notice (at a subconscious level)" both elements of the input and any "gap" that exists between those elements and the current state of their knowledge. This comparison process leads to acquisition. To this picture Schmidt and Frota (1986) added, contrary to Krashen's thinking, the hypothesis that the noticing is necessarily conscious – learners have to be aware of both the linguistic elements and the contrasts in order to benefit from their presence. Schmidt (1990) took the idea further, developing a more technical notion of noticing, which served as the basis for his Noticing Hypothesis – in order to benefit from input, learners must be aware of the relevant aspects of form in the input.

Noticing and the noticing hypothesis are referred to in a great deal of research on language instruction. Most of the work does not study them as such, though; the authors present them as background for the study or appeal to them as possible ways to understand the findings. A frequent but typically unrecognized problem in these references is that the meaning assigned to the word "noticing" shifts (see Truscott & Sharwood Smith, 2011). Schmidt (1990) was proposing a technical notion, with a relatively narrow meaning that excluded much, and probably most, of the things that researchers are interested in. Not surprisingly, then, there is a strong tendency in the literature to fall back on the ordinary language meaning of the word – awareness of something (anything). This research generally falls in the category of form focus, which I will briefly describe herein and then return to in Section 5.

A number of studies have specifically targeted the noticing hypothesis, usually with a recognition of the relatively narrow scope of "noticing." This means bringing in the accompanying notion of "awareness at the level of understanding" (see especially Schmidt, 1995), a type of awareness that was excluded from the hypothesis but is important in the context of second language instruction. An important addition to this research area is the application of eye-tracking methodology to determine what is or is not noticed (see Godfroid, 2020). Several reviews of noticing research are available (Gass, Behney, & Plonsky, 2020; Leow, 2015; Loewen, 2020; Loewen & Sato, 2017), reporting mixed findings. The issues involved in noticing and the research exploring it are large and complex, and I will not go into them here (for critical reviews, see Paradis, 2004, 2009; Truscott, 1998; Truscott & Sharwood Smith, 2011; VanPatten, 1994, 2015).

2.4 Implicit Knowledge and Implicit Learning

The notion of implicit (unconscious) knowledge/learning comes from cognitive psychology (e.g., Reber, 1993), particularly from experiments designed to test the possibility that people can learn things without being aware of what they learned or of the fact that they learned it – in other words, the possibility of implicit knowledge and implicit learning. In one design, participants see a row of lights in front of them flashing on and off in patterns that appear random but actually follow a pattern, of which they were not told. Their task is to respond to a given light going on by pressing the button corresponding to that light as quickly as possible. It was found that their reaction times gradually decreased, as if they were correctly anticipating the lights, but no conscious knowledge of the underlying pattern could be found by the experimenters, apparently indicating that they had acquired implicit knowledge, through implicit learning.

The other standard paradigm for implicit learning research, which is perhaps more relevant here, uses small artificial grammars, mimicking natural language grammar. Learners are presented with large numbers of "sentences" that can be produced by the grammar and then tested on how well they can judge if other instances, not previously shown to them, can or cannot be produced by that grammar. If they show some ability to do so, as they often do, and do not show any signs of conscious knowledge of how they are doing it, we have evidence of implicit learning and implicit knowledge.

The implicit learning literature is enormous (see especially Reber & Allen, 2022), and it has established beyond any reasonable doubt that implicit knowledge and learning are real and important. It is commonly conceptualized in terms of statistical learning, involving the frequencies of individual items and of the associations between them (see Rebuschat, 2022, for relevant discussion). This conception is developed especially in usage-based approaches (e.g., N. Ellis & Wulff, 2020). Unconscious knowledge and learning need not be seen in these terms, though. Universal grammar theorists, for example, typically take a very different view of unconscious knowledge and learning (see discussion).

The importance of implicit knowledge and learning for SLA has come to be widely recognized (see Lichtman & VanPatten, 2021; also the various papers in N. Ellis, 1994; Rebuschat, 2015; Sanz & Leow, 2011; VanPatten, Keating, & Wulff, 2020). The terms "implicit" and "explicit" now appear very widely in the research, notably in work on the effects of formal instruction. Researchers are interested in the effects of pedagogical interventions on the development of each type of knowledge and in the possible interactions of the two. For this purpose there is a need for means of distinguishing them in practice, a challenge that was taken up by R. Ellis (2005; see also R. Ellis et al., 2009). The criteria he offered are widely applied in research. But in this work, the role of input is at best a peripheral concern; its effects are tangled up with the effects of explicit instruction and other factors.[3] Another limitation of this work is that when implicit knowledge is acquired we do not know *how* it was acquired – implicitly or explicitly or through some combination of the two.

A substantial body of SLA research more directly addresses implicit learning and implicit knowledge, by studying them in controlled conditions (e.g., Brooks & Kempe, 2013; DeKeyser, 1995; Hama & Leow, 2010; Leung & Williams, 2011; Rogers, Révész, & Rebuschat, 2016; Williams, 2005). This work has made it reasonably clear that implicit learning does occur at least sometimes, though results are inconsistent. Perhaps more importantly, research of this type encounters serious issues of ecological validity, as it is difficult to pursue the questions in realistic contexts with realistic input and realistic measures of learning. We know that language-related knowledge can be implicitly acquired in laboratory settings, but what this tells us about actual language learning is open to dispute.

---

[3] I will return to this work in Section 5.

A significant issue for the study of implicit learning is whether it is influenced by explicit knowledge. We should expect there to be at least *some* influence of this sort, because of the potential of explicit knowledge for making input more comprehensible and its possible use by a learner to create virtual input (see Section 1). But the broader question is difficult to directly study. The problem of distinguishing implicit from explicit knowledge becomes severe when the latter has been automatized through extensive use and so is now used quickly and effortlessly and with little awareness. DeKeyser (2017; Suzuki & DeKeyser, 2017) has been especially concerned with this problem, as automatized explicit knowledge has a central place in his theory.

Suzuki and DeKeyser (2017) sought to empirically test the possibility that automatized explicit knowledge contributes to implicit knowledge. The measures that were used for automatized explicit knowledge are a possible issue in this study. The tests were timed grammaticality judgments, both written and aural, and a timed fill-in-the-blank task. The problem is that these tasks readily lend themselves to the use of implicit knowledge – people can easily perform them in their native language, for example, whether or not they have explicitly studied grammar. While the authors may be right that the tasks encouraged learners to focus on form and so encouraged the use of automatized explicit knowledge, a claim that implicit knowledge played no role in them, or that it had only a negligible role, seems doubtful. If the "explicit" tasks allowed even a fairly small role for implicit knowledge, then the weak relation that was found can be readily interpreted as a relation not between implicit knowledge and automatized explicit knowledge but rather between implicit knowledge and implicit knowledge. This is not, however, reason to close the book on research of this sort – challenges can be overcome.

2.5 Attention

Attention is an important topic in SLA, and the term appears throughout the literature. It is usually not treated as a distinct branch of its own, though, as most research on attention in SLA can also be classified as work on consciousness, noticing, implicit learning, input enhancement, focus on form, and possibly other topics as well.

Attention has been the focus of some theoretical work in the field. Gass' (1988) integrated model of SLA (see also Gass, Behney, & Plonsky, 2020, Ch. 17) gives attention a central place. Thinking on attention in SLA has been strongly influenced by Posner's theory (see Posner, 2012; Posner & Petersen, 1990; Posner & Rothbart, 1992), in which attention is split into three parts: *alertness* (or vigilance), *orientation* toward the stimulus, and *detection* of the target. Tomlin and Villa (1994) was essentially an application of the theory to SLA. Posner's work was also used by Robinson (1995), who interpreted noticing as detection (of a formal feature in the input) accompanied by rehearsal of that feature in working memory.

Much of Schmidt's writing on noticing (see especially Schmidt, 2001) focused on attention rather than consciousness, treating the two as essentially equivalent for his purposes. He argued that attention is necessary for all aspects of second language learning. While the claim has appeal, there is a problem, for this and other applications of attention to SLA. As Schmidt noted, the word "attention" has a variety of meanings in psychology. A consensus appears to exist in cognitive theory that there is in fact no single thing to which the term applies. It is a blanket term covering many different processes (e.g., Allport, 1993; Cohen, 2014; Nobre & Mesulam, 2014). For Nobre and Mesulam, the treatment of attention as a domain in itself has probably been a mistake; the features associated with "attention" should instead be studied as inherent parts of a wide variety of processes. There is also a danger of "attention," like "noticing" being used in a loose, ordinary-language sense and thereby losing what scientific foundation it has. These are general issues for work that invokes attention.

2.6 UG-based Research

Universal grammar (UG) is the innate knowledge of language hypothesized to underlie first language acquisition. The extension to second language acquisition constitutes a rich area of research (see Hawkins, 2019; Mitchell, Myles, & Marsden, 2019; Slabakova, Leal, Dudley, & Stack, 2020; White, 2020), but input in itself has not been a major concern in this research, a point brought out by Rankin and Unsworth (2016). From a UG perspective, the core of acquisition is establishing the values of various innately given *parameters*, determining word order for example. This is done through input, of course, but UG researchers have generally been more interested in showing the insufficiency of input for learning.

The acquisition process involves learners analyzing their input, on the basis of the innate principles and the L1, and making deductions from it about the nature of the target language. This is an "input as evidence" conception, the learner seen as a detective using evidence to solve a problem. So the way that input is analyzed or misanalyzed by learners, often reflecting L1 influence, is an important concern. Within this deductive approach, there is now a general recognition that frequency is important.

The bulk of the research that has been done within the UG perspective has assumed Chomskyan linguistic theory, in one form or another. But there is substantial variety among theories. Jackendoff's (1997, 2002) linguistic theory deviates considerably from Chomsky's thinking but remains very much within the UG camp. In SLA, the Modular Cognition Framework (e.g., Sharwood Smith & Truscott, 2014b; Truscott & Sharwood Smith, 2019), along with Carroll's (2001) Autonomous Induction Theory, assumes UG but is not committed to any particular linguistic theory. VanPatten's (2020) work similarly takes UG as a background assumption but focuses on the processing that produces the input to innate learning processes, leaving the nature of these processes as an open question.

2.7 Input Processing and Processing Instruction

VanPatten's (2009, 2017, 2020) Input Processing and Processing Instruction have spurred a considerable amount of research and are likely to continue to do so. VanPatten's work combines serious theoretical development, empirical research, and pedagogical application, all focused on input as the key to learning. The work is based on the fundamental point that learning depends on the way that learners process input.

The first issue then is how the processing occurs, and this is the domain of Input Processing (IP). VanPatten accepts the existence of universal grammar as a crucial part of acquisition, but does not give it a direct role in processing. Instead, separate processing mechanisms prepare the input for use by learning mechanisms, including UG. IP is about the processing mechanisms, for which a number of general principles are hypothesized. This understanding of input processing points to possibilities for pedagogical intervention (Processing Instruction, or PI). If the processing principles being used by learners are inappropriate for the language they are acquiring, the learning mechanisms will receive bad input, and learning will suffer as a result. If the processing procedures can be altered to a more appropriate form, learning will benefit. VanPatten stresses that this is not a method or an approach but rather a particular sort of intervention that can be used in a wide assortment of methods.

IP and PI have, again, stimulated a large body of experimental research (see VanPatten, 2009, 2017, for lengthy lists of references). As the goal of PI is to alter processing strategies, this is the focus of the research, and the main conclusions are that it is successful in this respect, both in absolute terms and relative to other types of intervention. Importantly, it is not claimed to improve learners' communicative ability.

2.8 Use of the Target Language to Teach Content

Use of the target language to teach content is an increasingly popular approach, appearing in a variety of forms. Considerable research has been carried out in classes of these types (e.g., Collier & Thomas, 2017; Feddermann, Möller, & Baumert, 2021; Graham, Choi, Davoodi, Razmeh, & Dixon, 2018; Martínez Agudo, 2020; Watzinger-Tharp, Rubio, & Tharp, 2018). In the SLA literature, the immersion research in Canada has played an especially important role (e.g., Collier, 1992; Swain, 1991). The approach tends to do well, though results are variable and it is difficult to draw general conclusions given the variety of pedagogical approaches that fall under this general heading. A common finding is that learners tend to do especially well in comprehension, often attaining native-like ability, but are somewhat less successful with productive skills. Proposed explanations for this limitation have included limited opportunities for production, narrow or impoverished input, and insufficient formal language instruction or insufficient integration of such instruction with content-based teaching (e.g., Snow, Met, & Genesee, 1989; Swain, 1985).

2.9 Interaction, Focus on Form, Output, and Corrective Feedback

The topics of this section are all major research areas in SLA and are intertwined with one another in theory, research, and pedagogy. They are also intertwined with input and so are relevant here, but input is not a central theme and the research does not seek to isolate or focus on input as such and so inferences about its nature or role are not straightforward.

The role of interaction in second language learning constitutes a particularly rich research area, or perhaps a cluster of rich research areas. The target of this work, interaction, is a coherent package of input, output, and feedback, within a communicative context in which meaning is negotiated between the participants. While the role of input is not isolated, most will agree that it is central. The primary motivation for Long's early, influential proposals was in fact the idea that interaction should contribute greatly to the goal of providing comprehensible input (see Long, 1983, 1996).

There does not seem to be any dispute regarding the value of the overall package for acquisition. This value can probably be accommodated in all major theories, and interaction research can potentially contribute to the development of SLA theory quite broadly. Probably the bulk of the research falls under the heading of focus on form, or more loosely form focus. It should be stressed that, despite the name, form focus as it is commonly recommended now treats meaning as primary, placing the form focus in the context of meaningful activities.

All the topics considered in this section are closely associated with work on consciousness and attention, described earlier, notably work on noticing and the implicit-explicit distinction. The sources cited there are also relevant here. Extensive review and discussion of research in this group of interrelated topics can be found in Gass, Behney, and Plonsky (2020), Gass and Mackey (2020), and Loewen and Sato (2017).

2.10 Input and the Development of Phonology

In much SLA work, including work on input, phonology tends to be taken for granted. But phonological processing and learning is in a sense the most fundamental issue, as all spoken input – and any resulting acquisition – begins with perception of the sounds. A substantial body of research exists on the development of second language phonology, and much of it involves input (e.g., Bohn & Munro, 2007; Flege, 2009; Kennedy & Trofimovich, 2017; Piske & Young-Scholten, 2009; White, Titone, Genesee, & Steinhauer, 2017; Young-Scholten, 1996).

Largely the same issues arise here as in other areas of input research. First, the importance of input for development is acknowledged, while research is directed to the question of *how* important it is relative to the other factors, such as the L1 and the age of the learner. The role of consciousness and attention is a common theme in the research, frequently cast in terms of noticing. This concern is naturally accompanied by applications to pedagogy, including issues of output practice, explicit instruction, interaction, and input enhancement. The question of innateness is also pursued – the possible innateness of principles involving hierarchies and markedness as well as stages of development possibly arising from innate constraints (Universal Phonology).

2.11 Conclusion

Identifying distinct branches of research on input is, again, difficult and somewhat arbitrary. We might add research done within given SLA theories, like O'Grady's (2005, 2015) emergentist model, MacWhinney's (Unified) Competition Model (e.g., MacWhinney, 2012), and Pienemann's Processability Theory (see Pienemann & Lenzing, 2020). I have left out these and other theories because, while their treatment of input is important, the research done within them is rarely focused on it. I have also left out most research done within socially or culturally oriented theories because "input," as a cognitive, information-processing concept, is not widely accepted in these areas and does not play a major role in the research. Likewise for the Complex Dynamic Systems Theory developed for SLA by Larsen-Freeman (2020), who rejects the term "input" as dehumanizing (among other objections).

3 What Are the Implications for SLA?

The term "SLA" can be understood in a broad sense to include all work related to the acquisition of languages beyond the first. But here it will be used in the narrower sense of theory and research attempting to establish a scientific understanding of the subject, as distinct from efforts to establish useful guidelines for instruction. The latter will be considered in Section 5. The question at this point is what lessons might be drawn from existing research for the development of a scientific understanding of SLA. The discussion will be relatively brief, its purpose being to offer a perspective on previous sections and an introduction to Sections 4 and 5, where most of the topics will be explored in more depth.

The first lesson I would draw is that caution is required. While much has been learned, it would be bold to claim that we have achieved a general understanding or that commonly accepted ideas are now on solid ground. At this point, lack of consensus is not a problem; it is an honest recognition that while we may be on the road to real understanding, the destination is not yet in sight. That said, a number of significant points can be drawn from the research.

First, input is not just something out there. To understand the subject, we have to recognize that what is out there goes through an elaborate construction process on its way to influencing language learning. Input is best seen as the name for this process, or as the general topic of how what is out there affects what is in the learner's head. This topic might well be characterized simply as perception – the study of how perception works in the case of second language learning.

Perhaps the most prominent theme in current research is the importance of implicit knowledge acquired in implicit learning, through input processing. There does not seem to be any serious dispute any longer regarding the existence of two distinct types of knowledge/learning, or the primacy of the type that is commonly characterized as implicit. The explicit variety of knowledge, obtained through other means, has value for learning and for use but is very much secondary – the extent of its value is a significant topic for continuing research.

Given the prominent role of implicit knowledge and learning and their contrast with explicit knowledge and learning, a crucial question is whether this is in fact the right way to draw the distinctions. Should theory and research findings be recast in terms of the procedural-declarative distinction? This would mean drawing the lines without reference to consciousness and then asking to what extent and in what ways consciousness is associated with the actual systems. I will consider this and related theoretical issues in Section 4.

There has been extensive work on the effects of instruction on implicit and explicit knowledge, including efforts to separate them using different types of tests. While claims are made about benefits for implicit knowledge, it is not easy to see how benefits from relatively brief, explicit treatments can be explained in terms of the gradual statistical tallying that is commonly taken to underlie the development of implicit knowledge. This suggests either that it is not implicit knowledge that is being acquired or that different conceptions of implicit knowledge and/or learning are needed.

Efforts to influence (implicit) learning by directing learners' attention to features of their input have not fared particularly well in the research, a point that is far from conclusive but should raise some doubts about the value of attention to form and awareness of form. There is good reason to think that VanPatten's processing instruction helps learners deal with problematic input, but the effects on language acquisition itself remain uncertain.

Continuing development and testing of theoretical approaches is necessary. Linguistic theory plays a crucial role – we cannot understand how knowledge is acquired without understanding what that knowledge looks like. It should not be forgotten, though, that there is not, as of yet, any definitive answer to the question of what language really looks like. The view of language on which a given approach rests is always open to challenge. Research and theory in psychology are also of great value and should continue to play an important role, though their application is by no means straightforward, nor are particular applications uncontroversial. The contrast between technical meanings of terms and their intuitive, ordinary-language meanings must be recognized.

One fundamental issue is not receiving anything like the attention it deserves. This is the foundational issue for a theory of learning: How do the proposed learning mechanisms know what to look for in their input? Our remarkable ability to make sense of what we encounter requires an account of how these mechanisms manage to focus in on the things they need without getting lost in the vast complexity of the world in which those things are embedded. This issue brings out the need for a stronger theoretical grounding.

An increased concern with theory means seriously pursuing questions that are fundamental for an understanding of input but are rarely if ever addressed, or even recognized as questions. Consciousness of input and attention to input are central issues in SLA. But input is a multi-stage construction process rather than a thing in itself. So what exactly does it mean to be conscious of input, or to attend to it? To pursue the question, we need both a more refined concept of input and clear ideas of how consciousness and attention fit into the perceptual process that is input. In their absence, "conscious of input" is vague or ambiguous; for serious study of input, this is not good enough.

4 An Integrated View of Input in Second Language Learning

It is time to put things together into what will hopefully be a coherent picture of input and its place in second language learning, one that will, among other things, address the fundamental questions just raised. The picture will be a cognitive one, placing the topics in the context of cognitive research and theory. More specifically, it will be my own picture, based on the Modular Cognition Framework (MCF; e.g., Sharwood Smith & Truscott, 2014b; Truscott, 2022b; Truscott & Sharwood Smith, 2019).

4.1 Input, Perception, and Bird Calls

The first and most important topic is perception. And the first and most important thing to understand about perception, as noted in Section 1, is that it is not a process of taking what is outside and bringing it inside. It is about *constructing* internal representations of experiences. The representation constructed in this way is connected to already stored objects, and associated with related knowledge and with emotion. The end result of the process is the scene that we perceive, a representation of what is outside but by no means a simple internalization of it. The process is depicted in Figure 1.

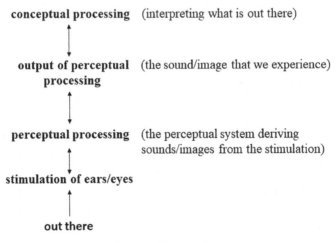

Figure 1 Perception

The figure applies to all the senses, individually, so "perceptual" could be read as "visual," producing images, or as "auditory," producing sounds, among other possibilities. The perceptual *output* stage is the border between perceptual systems and higher level systems, particularly the conceptual. It represents the ultimate product of the perceptual processing – the sounds and images, that is – and is thus the immediate input to conceptual processing, which gives meaning to those products.

The existence of distinct perceptual and conceptual systems can be seen in two different types of *agnosias* (see Behrmann, 2010; Griffiths, 2010). Damage to parts of the brain that deal with conceptual processing can leave you with a clear image or sound but no idea what it is that you are seeing or hearing (*associative* agnosia). Damage to lower areas, on the other hand, can prevent the formation of a clear image or sound, making it difficult or impossible for the later processes to interpret it (*apperceptive* agnosia). Note also the bidirectional arrows in the figure, expressing the extensive interaction that occurs among the different systems.

The perceptual process is perhaps best understood through examples. Consider first the case of hearing a sound which you, being an expert on bird vocalization, recognize as the call of a marbled godwit. The air coming from the bird disturbs the air around you, producing vibrations in your ears. The auditory system constructs from these vibrations a representation for the sound "out there" and matches it with already existing sound representations. The candidates for this matching are contained in the store of sounds you experienced in the past – what can be called auditory output representations – one of which is the call of the marbled godwit. When this representation is activated, it activates a connected representation in the conceptual system, MARBLED GODWIT CALL. You have then perceived the call.

What about a bird call that you don't already know? If you have never heard it before, there is no representation of its sound in the auditory store or its interpretation in the conceptual store. Auditory processing therefore creates a new auditory representation, using sounds that are already present. This new representation will then be connected to a conceptual representation. If you witness the bird making that sound, this new representation will specify that particular bird (the alternative would be a generic "bird sound" representation). You have then *learned* the sound that a particular bird makes.

We can now ask about the input to this learning. What exactly *is* it? One possibility is to identify the input as what is out there in the world, since that is what started the whole thing and is what the new representations are representing. But the new auditory representation that you acquire is the product of an elaborate construction process involving a number of intermediate representations (not shown in the figure), so maybe the input has to be placed between the bird and the output representation. The new conceptual representation is based on the auditory representation,[4] so maybe the auditory representation should be considered the real input to learning. Nothing is particularly wrong with any of these options – apart from the fact that each deals with only one part of the process. So maybe we should say the input is the whole perceptual process.

How we choose to apply the term "input" is rather arbitrary. The important point is that it is inseparable from the construction process and the individual representations involved in it. Also worth noting is the contribution of the visual experience, seeing the bird making noise. We could say it is part of the input, or that it provides the information needed to establish the conceptual representation; in other words, that it makes the input comprehensible.

4.2 Input, Perception, and Language

When we go from this simple example to language and language learning, extra complications come in, lots of them. But the basics of perception remain the same. What is distinctive about human language is that it adds a very rich means of connecting sounds (the output of auditory processing, that is) to concepts, allowing us to express an unlimited number of possible ideas and, more immediately relevant, to understand someone else's expression of them. Figure 2 portrays the perception of language sounds (or written words).

ᵻ Suppose during the bird noise someone says "That's a marbled godwit."[5] This event, out there, causes vibrations in your ears, which trigger auditory processing, culminating in an output representation of the sound of the utterance. To this point perception is essentially the same process as in the previous examples. If you didn't understand English it could be almost entirely the same process: A conceptual representation would be directly constructed for the auditory output, perhaps consisting of the information that the sound was "something in English," comparable to the concept in the previous example that you were hearing some sort of bird call.

Things are more interesting, though, if you *can* understand English or, especially, if you are learning to understand it. In this case processing will take a left turn at the auditory output. Specifically linguistic processes will deal with the sounds, constructing a sentence from them. Conceptual processes then form an interpretation for this sentence, just as they interpreted the bird sound

---

[4] Note that when the sound is mis-heard, resulting in an auditory representation that does not accurately represent what is out there, it is this inappropriate representation that serves as the basis for conceptual learning.

[5] This is another means of making the bird input comprehensible, by the way.

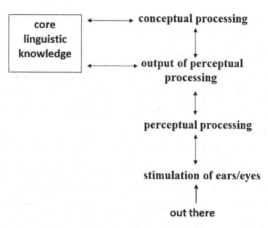

Figure 2 Perception and language

(though with far greater complexity, of course). This linguistic-conceptual processing is carried out by systems having their own specializations, using the output of processing by the perceptual systems.

Note that the linguistic box in Figure 2 is labeled core linguistic knowledge rather than just linguistic knowledge. This is because of the non-monolithic nature of language described in Section 1. The core is the portion that is specifically responsible for the rich sound-meaning connections that make human language special.

At this point we can ask again: Where is "input" in this picture? The term could be used to refer to what is out there, or to any or all of the intermediate steps in the processing, or to the process as a whole. All can be useful ways of talking about the phenomena. Problems arise when we think that input is some real "thing" that needs to be pinned down. The important point is that input is inseparable from perception and therefore shows all the general characteristics of the perceptual process: multi-step construction carried out in terms of already-existing representations (linguistic and other). And it is this construction process that sets up learning and makes it possible.

4.3 Language in the Mind

The previous examples referred to different components in the mind – auditory, visual, conceptual, core linguistic – reflecting the fact that a complex system, such as the human mind, is necessarily composed of interacting parts. These parts represent different types of knowledge, encoded in different ways, associated with different types of processing. In order for the system to function properly, these various aspects of its operations must be segregated in some sense, so that a new face for example is processed as a face and not as an algebraic formula or a string of phonetic features or some mixture of these and other types of knowledge. In the brain this can mean that faces occupy a particular region[6] and/or that face representations have especially strong connections to one another and to the lower-level visual features that are used in their construction. A central question for research and theory is the nature of the segregation: What exactly *are* the parts of the system? How do they interact?

The parts, whatever they may be, are often referred to as *modules*, and when we seek to understand their nature we are studying *modularity*. Many would avoid these terms, but in a broad sense everyone accepts the idea behind them. The system simply could not work without some sort of segregation of the knowledge types and the processes that construct and work with each type. Important disagreements involve the nature and extent of the segregation and especially the role of our genes – to what extent and in what sense are the modules innately determined? I will return to these questions herein.

When we talk about parts of the system, language is naturally taken to be one of those parts. Linguistic input is necessarily encoded in terms of linguistic features, and stored in a linguistic place. I use the term "place" in a loose sense, simply to mean that some sort of segregation exists. Given the non-monolithic character of language described earlier, it is actually more accurate to speak of place*s* rather than place. Of particular importance here is core language, the knowledge that allows rich connections between sounds and meanings, as pictured in Figure 2.

What happens when there are two languages in one head? A second language has, necessarily, all the components of a first language. We also know that a bilingual's two languages are intertwined, as seen in the ability of bilinguals to smoothly switch between their languages and merge them in rule-governed ways within a conversation. Research has shown that when a bilingual is using one language, relevant elements of the other are automatically activated, meaning primed for use (for reviews, see Brysbaert & Duyck, 2010; de Groot & Starreveld, 2015; Kroll, Gullifer, McClain, Rossi, & Martín, 2015; Schwartz, 2015). A reasonable interpretation is that the two languages are stored in the same "places."

The conceptual system has a special status. Unlike visual, auditory, or linguistic systems, it is not dedicated to one type of function but is rather a very general, multi-function system, which is to say we can acquire abstract conceptual knowledge of virtually any type. What all the types have in common is that they are represented in the abstract, *domain-general* format of concepts.

---

[6] They do, in fact; e.g., Kanwisher, McDermott, and Chun (1997).

Readers familiar with research on memory might note the resemblance to *declarative* memory – the kind of knowledge that we can, at least in principle, describe and talk about. I will return to this point later.

The conceptual system's ability to acquire abstract knowledge on virtually anything naturally extends to language. The knowledge acquired in a linguistics class is an obvious example. More interesting here is the knowledge acquired in a grammar-oriented second language class. Knowing that the past participle verb form is used in English passive sentences is not fundamentally different from knowing that Ouagadougou is the capital of Burkina Faso. Both are instances of abstract conceptual knowledge. What makes the language-related knowledge different is simply that it is about language. This is the metalinguistic knowledge described earlier (1.1)

4.4 Changing the Places in the Mind: Learning

Learning from input means making changes in the places where the processing occurs. Returning to the bird-call examples, if you were one of those benighted individuals who had never heard of a marbled godwit, the linguistic-conceptual processes would form new representations – linguistic and conceptual – to accommodate the new word. This is what sets up learning.

In the account developed in the Modular Cognition Framework, this processing simply *is* learning (see Sharwood Smith & Truscott, 2014b; Truscott & Sharwood Smith, 2004). Importantly, there is no conflict here with the idea (see 1.3) that learning means forming internal models of the external world. The claim is that the products of the perceptual (input) process directly, automatically contribute to the developing models, as opposed to the idea that they are first submitted to a separate set of learning processes, which then make the appropriate adjustments in the models. From this point onward, I will assume this parsimonious approach to learning.

Input and the acquisition that results from it should thus be understood as the interaction of processing in the perceptual system itself with the processing in the higher-level systems. The former produces the perceptual output representations which the latter then uses to establish linguistic representations of what is out there. In some cases, the higher-level processing is just a matter of activating (and thereby strengthening) what is already present, as when the learner hears "Good morning" or "How are you?" for the hundredth time. More often, it would mean representing a novel sentence by combining established representations in an already-established manner – when all the words and structures are known but have never been encountered together before.

Most interesting is the case in which the high-level processes are faced with a perceptual output representation that they cannot handle in either of these ways. This might mean a new word (*marbled godwit*), a new grammatical element (*-ed*), a new structure (passive), or perhaps something much more subtle, depending on one's preferred linguistic theory. To form adequate overall representations for this novel perceptual output, the high-level processes will have to establish new representations. These new elements are then part of the interlanguage. If they prove useful in subsequent processing, their continuing use will strengthen them; if not, they will gradually become irrelevant as they get weaker and their rivals get stronger.

A principle that is generally accepted, but not so generally discussed or analyzed, is that understanding the meaning of the input is important for learning from that input. If you don't understand what "That's a marbled godwit" means, it is difficult to learn the word "marbled godwit." If you are going to learn the English past tense marker from input like "Chris talked," it is very helpful to know that the talking occurred in the past. In terms of Figure 2, understanding the input means having an appropriate conceptual representation of it, which can then be used in linguistic processing – and therefore linguistic learning.

4.5 Input, Perception, and Consciousness

Ideas about consciousness play a central role in SLA, as can be seen in the prominence of the terms *noticing, noticing the gap, implicit*, and *explicit*. Even when consciousness is not mentioned, it is often present in the background, in discussions of teaching or correcting language form. To understand input and its role in SLA, we have to look in some depth at consciousness, especially its place in perception.

When we hear (or read) a word or a sentence, what things can be part of the conscious experience and what things cannot? We are certainly aware of the sound; in normal circumstances it is very difficult *not* to be aware of it. Recall, though, that the sounds we hear are the product of the complex, multi-step construction process that is perception. This process itself is clearly not part of the conscious experience. In terms of the earlier depiction of perception, Figure 2, repeated here with a small addition as Figure 3, the conscious experience is of perceptual output but does not include what comes before that stage. The dashed arrow will be explained shortly.

What about the purely linguistic parts of Figure 3? Are they part of our conscious experience? To anyone who has studied linguistic theory and its complex, unintuitive, and constantly disputed theories of phonology and syntax,

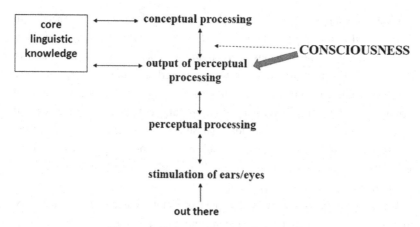

Figure 3 Consciousness and perception

it should be clear that the answer is no. Similarly, a language teacher struggling to answer students' questions about grammar knows that we cannot find the abstract principles underlying language simply by examining our conscious experience. We can learn the principles presented in textbooks, and possibly infer some for ourselves, but they are not there in the conscious experience of hearing language.

This brings us to the trickiest part – the conceptual component: Can we be conscious of the meaning of what we hear? The best answer is "no, but . . . ." Concepts are abstract, which means they are a step removed from direct experience. Consider, for example, the concept of MUSIC. What would an experience of the abstract concept be like? When we listen to music, or hear the word "music," the conscious experience is of some *particular* music, possibly with visual images of musical notes or of a band or a musical instrument. But these things are not MUSIC; they are perceptual elements associated with it. The same considerations apply to more concrete cases, like CUP. An abstract cup has no particular size, shape, color, and so on. But any cup you can experience or imagine does have particular features of this sort. The experiences are perceptual rather than conceptual. This is the *perceptual bias of conscious-ness* (Baars, 1988, 1997).

But, when we hear the words "cup" or "music," there is certainly a sense in which we *feel* that we are aware of their meaning, even if it is difficult to find anything in the conscious experience that could be called a meaning. There is a feeling that the sounds are making sense – that they are connecting properly to concepts – and that we can express the meaning if we choose to. This feeling is shown perhaps most clearly by its absence when we hear something said in an unfamiliar language. In the two cases we see the contrast between the experience of hearing sounds and the experience of hearing *interpreted* sounds. The apparent conclusion is that the conceptual, meaning level is not directly part of conscious experience but is always lurking in the background, coloring the perceptual experiences. This is expressed in Figure 3 by the dashed arrow.

Putting all this together, the perceptual output level is where consciousness is found, at the border between perceptual and conceptual processing.[7] The senses present us with a picture of the world around us, which other components of the mind interpret and use for their own purposes. Our conscious experience is of this picture.[8] Awareness of the perceptual output representation is thus a normal part of perception, including the perception that constitutes second language input. When we are aware of "input," it is specifically a perceptual output representation that we are aware of – a representation that is currently dominating processing at the perceptual output level. To this picture we have to add *indirect* awareness of meaning, in the form of a conceptual representation of the input.

4.6 Input, Consciousness, and Learning

We can now address an issue that has always been at the heart of SLA, if often implicitly: To what extent and in what ways is learning a conscious process? In particular, what do learners need to be aware of in regard to input? What does it mean to be aware of these things?

First, do learners need to be aware of "**input**"? There is, again, no "thing" called input, so this question can only be answered in terms of the components of the perceptual process, as this process is what constitutes input. Returning to Figure 3, awareness of input necessarily means awareness of **perceptual output** representations, because this is where consciousness resides. This is to say learners are aware of the sound of the voices they are hearing, or of the images of what they are reading. A claim that this sort of awareness is unnecessary would amount to a claim that we can learn language while we are asleep or fully absorbed in an unrelated task, and I know of no one in the field who would make such a claim. Thus, awareness of "input" itself is not a topic of research or discussion in SLA.[9] The issue is not learners' awareness of input but rather their awareness of particular aspects of the input, aspects of its linguistic form in particular. This issue will be addressed shortly.

---

[7] Compare Jackendoff's (1987) Intermediate Levels theory of consciousness. Jackendoff (2012) also presents what is probably the best available account of the way that concepts are and are not involved in conscious experience.

[8] To simplify the discussion, I have avoided the important topic of affective consciousness (see Truscott, 2015).

[9] The same point applies to *attention* to input.

Perceptual output takes on special significance here because, in addition to being the locus of consciousness, it serves as the material for processing in the conceptual and linguistic systems, including the novel processing that constitutes learning, as shown in Figure 3. This is why awareness of input is so strongly associated with learning in general – why we learn little or nothing from "input" that occurs while we are asleep or distracted. If an input sentence does not come to dominate at the level of perceptual output, then (a) we are not aware of it, and (b) linguistic and conceptual processing can do little or nothing with it; in other words, it does not constitute intake.

Do learners need to be aware of **meaning** in order to learn from input? This question has not, to my knowledge, generated any debate, and is rarely discussed. It appears to be taken for granted that such awareness is either necessary or extremely valuable, though what exactly it means to be aware of meaning has never been made clear. In terms of the previous discussion, what it means is indirect awareness of conceptual representations – awareness that the perceptual output sounds (or images) are appropriately connecting up to conceptual representations, making them meaningful.

Thus, awareness of perceptual output and its connections to conceptual representations is a normal and probably essential part of learning from input, no matter how that learning occurs. One implication is that the distinction between implicit and explicit learning is not about awareness of input as such, as both involve awareness of perceptual output. The line between them must be drawn elsewhere, a point to which I will return shortly.

In SLA discussions of consciousness, the subject of interest, and the source of controversy, is the remaining question: Do learners need to be aware of **linguistic form** in their input, things like past tense endings or passive forms or word order? When the conscious experience is of a sentence itself but not of the fact that it contains a subject and a verb or that the two are appearing in that order, what can the higher-level processes do with this implicit linguistic information? If the sentence is in a language that we already know, the answer is clear: They can use it, quickly and efficiently, to construct linguistic representations of the sentence and determine its meaning. To successfully process and understand the sentence you just read, for example, you do not have to be consciously thinking of subjects and verbs or their order in the sentence. You use the implicit information automatically and unconsciously. But what about someone who is just learning the language? Does learning require them to be aware of subjects and verbs and such?

To address the question, we first have to ask what it means to be aware of language form in the input (see Truscott & Sharwood Smith, 2011, for more detailed discussion of these matters). As described in Section 1, knowledge of language comes in two very different varieties – linguistic and metalinguistic. Linguistic knowledge makes up the core linguistic system of Figure 3, while metalinguistic knowledge is found in the conceptual system. As argued earlier, we cannot be aware of the linguistic representations but can be aware, indirectly, of conceptual representations, including those of metalinguistic knowledge.

What, then, does it mean to be aware of subjects and verbs and such in the input? It means being aware of conceptual, metalinguistic representations, like SUBJECT, VERB, or PAST TENSE. And in order for one of these to be (indirectly) part of conscious experience, it must be connected to a perceptual representation that is currently dominating perceptual output. Thus, *awareness of language form is awareness of a perceptual output representation connected to a conceptual, metalinguistic representation of the form*. The simplest kind of example is awareness of the [t] sound in "walked" with its connection to a conceptual representation, namely PAST TENSE.

At this point we are no longer talking about the input sentence itself but rather a follow-up representation that isolates one portion or aspect of it. For the case of past tense [t] again, this means a perceptual representation specifically of the [t] portion of the original input, connected to the conceptual representation PAST TENSE. Awareness of these things is awareness that [t] is a past tense form. This awareness might be accompanied, perhaps fleetingly, by the experience of the voice in the head saying "past tense" or of images related to it.

A somewhat different case involves awareness of word order – awareness that the subject is preceding the verb, for example. If the input sentence is "The student walks to school every day," the follow-up perceptual representation might be "The student walks," which would be connected to a conceptual representation such as SUBJECT-VERB or SUBJECT PRECEDES VERB. We then have awareness of the information that "The student walks" is an instance of subject preceding verb, possibly with a conscious experience of the voice in the head or of related images. This explicit processing might lead to additional conceptual processing that yields a more abstract metalinguistic representation like SUBJECT PRECEDES VERB IN ENGLISH.

Implicit learning from input is in a sense much simpler than explicit learning. The learner just consciously hears and understands the sentence. Awareness is simply of the interpreted sounds of this sentence – the perceptual output representation.

How then does the awareness of linguistic form, as characterized here, relate to the development of the different types of knowledge of language? Development of the linguistic system, first, is generally recognized to be predominantly if not entirely implicit. Unconscious processes use the interpreted perceptual representation, as is, to make changes in the linguistic

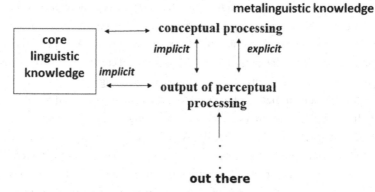

Figure 4 Implicit and explicit learning from input

system – those changes that are needed to adequately represent the current input. Through many such instances of input processing, the learner gradually acquires the ability to use aspects of form automatically, and is never aware of the linguistic knowledge.

In contrast, metalinguistic knowledge, being simply conceptual knowledge that is about language, is typically the product of explicit learning. The previous descriptions of past tense and word order offer paradigm cases of the acquisition of metalinguistic knowledge (or at least the early stages of the process). But a role for implicit learning is also quite plausible – there is no apparent reason why it should not be possible. Findings of implicit learning under controlled laboratory conditions might well be interpreted in these terms, as the unconscious acquisition of conceptual knowledge about language, distinct from development of the linguistic system itself. The important point, for practical purposes, is that this learning is done without the linguistic specialization found in the linguistic system, and its products are therefore likely to be a pale imitation of genuine linguistic knowledge.

The conception of learning presented here, both implicit and explicit, is depicted in Figure 4. We could perhaps place a small question mark on the vertical "implicit" arrow (see the following section for related discussion).

4.7 Rethinking the Implicit-Explicit Distinction

To this point I have followed standard practice in SLA by assuming that the implicit-explicit distinction is a fundamental divide in terms of knowledge and learning types. But this assumption is in dispute (in the SLA context, see

Ullman, 2016, 2020).[10] The original dichotomy of learning and memory types – and the one that best fits with what we know about the brain – was not implicit vs. explicit but rather procedural vs. declarative (see Squire & Wixted, 2011), in other words the ability to do things, physical and mental, vs. factual knowledge. For SLA, this distinction offers a good match with the distinction between the linguistic system, which underlies competent use of a language, and the conceptual system with its metalinguistic knowledge. Conceptual and declarative, as they are commonly understood, are not easily distinguished.

Taking procedural (linguistic) vs. declarative (metalinguistic) as the fundamental divide, we can then return to the question of consciousness in language learning, with the same answer offered earlier (see Figure 4). Neurobiological findings (see Chun, 2000; Henke, 2010; Schendan, Searl, Melrose, & Stern, 2003; Ullman, 2020) suggest that procedural knowledge and learning are always implicit while their declarative counterparts tend to be explicit but can also be implicit. This is to say, again, that development of the linguistic system is an entirely implicit process while metalinguistic knowledge is typically, but not necessarily, obtained explicitly.

4.8 "Input" Revisited and Expanded

In thinking about how we interpret things out there, it is natural to focus narrowly on the object or event that we are mainly interested in, like the sound of a bird call or the utterance that is being processed. But perception is more than this, and a treatment of input should recognize this additional complexity. For the case of second language learning, the non-monolithic character of language dictates a broadened view of this sort. Knowledge of language includes a number of components that are not strictly linguistic, each of which is acquired through input and so should be considered a part of the input.

An important part of knowing a language, for example, is knowing how to use it appropriately in given contexts, involving, among other things, a particular speaker, a particular physical setting, and previous utterances and actions. These contexts are part of the perception (the input) and so become connected to the more strictly linguistic parts of the acquired knowledge, creating a composite "language in context" representation. In addition to context, perception also involves the person's attitude toward what he/she is perceiving – the value attached to it and the emotion that it evokes. To these

---

[10] Rethinking the implicit-explicit distinction in SLA may be to some extent a matter of clarifying terminology. In principle, "implicit" *means* unconscious, but it is not always used this way (e.g., R. Ellis et al., 2009), and it is not always clear what meaning is intended.

can be added the *goal* of the speaker. All of these become connected to the more strictly linguistic knowledge, through input. We thus need a broadened notion of input to include all these elements.

This broadening of "input" is one of the ways in which a social account of second language learning, dealing with such things as contexts and goals, interfaces with a cognitive account. It is naturally accommodated in the Modular Cognition Framework through its concept of *internal context* (Sharwood Smith, 2021; Truscott & Sharwood Smith, 2019).

4.9 How Is Learning Possible? The Issue of Innate Knowledge

Input, in the sense of what is out there, is embedded in the world. And the world is very complex. Our senses are constantly assaulted by an essentially infinite variety of sights and sounds (to say nothing of smells, tastes, and feels), from which we somehow derive our rich knowledge, including knowledge of language. More accurately, our implicit learning mechanisms derive our rich knowledge of language. They somehow manage to pick out, from the vast complexity of the world, exactly those things that are needed for their task and use them to create something remarkable – a human language. How is this possible?

An immediate response is that the implicit mechanisms identify patterns in the information they are receiving from the senses (the input) and in effect reproduce these patterns internally. But while this idea has considerable intuitive appeal, it still leaves us with the question of how the relevant patterns can be extracted from the vast complexity of the world. Patterns are relations among given elements, and the number of possible elements and possible relations among them is astronomical. How do the learning mechanisms know what counts as a relevant element for their current task? How do they know what kinds of relations to look for among those elements?

To get a feel for the enormity of the task, consider some of the information that is contained in a simple sentence like the following.

The man noticed a dog in the yard behind the fence.

The sentence contains exactly three instances of the word *the*; five other words, with a total of six syllables, appear between the first two instances, and two words, with a total of three syllables, appear between the second and third; the first word in the sentence begins with a voiced consonant while the last word begins and ends with an unvoiced consonant; the past tense marker appears on a verb that has two syllables, the first of which is stressed; an indefinite article immediately follows the past tense marker; the object of each preposition appearing in the sentence is headed by a singular, inanimate, countable noun and so on.

Also relevant is the listener's background knowledge about the referents, for example, that the agent of the sentence ("the man") is understood to be an Armenian businessman of medium build with a receding hairline, that the dog might well be a small terrier belonging to the good-natured gentleman down the street, and so on. Also of potential significance is that the person who uttered this sentence was seated at the time, was wearing a light blue shirt with a stain on the right sleeve near the elbow, and had a surprisingly low voice which rose in volume at a point in the middle of the sentence.

A general, unconstrained learning mechanism would have to keep track of all such information in the input it receives, maintaining a record of how often each item co-occurs with each of the others, in combinations of all possible sizes. It would also have to correlate each item and each combination with the current temperature in the room, the scrambled eggs which the learner had for breakfast, and the phase of the moon. And this, of course, is just a tiny sampling of the possibilities that would have to be considered.

This is the problem of *computational tractability* (see Carruthers, 2006; Fodor, 1983). A learning mechanism that is not receiving strong guidance on what to look for will have so many possibilities to consider that its task becomes impossible. There has to be something that tells it to look for certain things in the input and disregard everything else and to consider only certain possibilities for the way those things can be associated. This is the essential, foundational element for a theory of learning.

What then is it that is guiding the learning? The approach I adopt here, based on the Modular Cognition Framework, is a UG approach. As such, it hypothesizes that language learning – specifically, learning of core linguistic knowledge – is a narrow, highly constrained process. Patterns in the input are no less real or important in this approach, but the basic elements that make up those patterns are identified in advance, as are the possible ways in which they can be related. The vast majority of possibilities are thus ruled out from the beginning, making the task manageable. In terms of the discussion in 4.7, UG is a system of constraints that evolved to facilitate the procedural learning of language. Such domain-specific adaptations seem quite natural with functions that have proven important for survival, functions like language.

Alternative approaches, commonly called "usage-based" now, hypothesize that learning is carried out by simple, general mechanisms that make no use of specifically linguistic knowledge (see for example N. Ellis & Wulff, 2020). But in order for such mechanisms to learn language (or anything else) there still have to be constraints that focus them on particular items and on particular ways those items can be connected. The foundational challenge for such an approach is in establishing what these constraints are and where they come from – without taking any specifically linguistic information as a given. This is a large challenge, and one which has not, to my knowledge, been confronted by SLA theorists. When simple, general learning mechanisms are offered as explanations for language learning, we have to ask how much of the simplicity and generality comes from setting aside the foundational issue faced by all theories of learning.

5 What Are the Implications for Pedagogy?

Previous sections characterized input and its relation to learning, including the place of consciousness in the process. With this understanding as background, we can now take up the question of pedagogy. Given what we know about input and the types of knowledge and processes related to it, what is the best way to approach second language instruction?

5.1 The Choices

It is now widely accepted among SLA researchers that natural, implicit processes, operating through input processing, are the heart of second language acquisition (e.g., Lichtman & VanPatten, 2021; and the various chapters in VanPatten, Keating, & Wulff, 2020). The apparent implication is that these processes should be the central concern in language teaching. While traditional grammar-based instruction remains prominent in practice, it now receives little respect in the SLA literature. This shift is well illustrated by the fact that the most prominent advocate of such instruction, Robert DeKeyser, is now quite cautious in his statements about it (see DeKeyser, 2020). He accepts the existence and importance of implicit learning and places strong limits on the applicability of his own theory, which represents the underlying logic of traditional grammar-based instruction.

This does not mean that nothing is learned in traditional grammar teaching. As described earlier, the conceptual system has the ability to (effortfully) acquire knowledge (declarative knowledge, that is) on virtually any subject, including language. It can learn the meanings of words or symbols and memorize rules for combining them. In other words, it can treat linguistic symbols like other symbols (mathematical, for example). This is what traditional grammar teaching and learning are about. But the conceptual system's lack of linguistic specialization greatly limits the extent of its success in any given area, notably in language. If we are satisfied with developing in students the most basic ability to say things in the language, slowly and effortfully (and often wrongly), this kind of learning can be worthwhile. But to go beyond this, we have to go beyond conceptual learning and focus on implicit development of the linguistic system.

So, input and the natural acquisition processes that rely on it are at the heart of second language learning. This recognition leaves us with two general approaches to the use of input in teaching:

1. Trust the natural acquisition processes: facilitate their workings by providing appropriate sources of input, helping learners understand it, and making the experience as pleasurable as possible;
2. Try to assist the natural processes through form-focused interventions: direct those processes to selected aspects of form in the input; select input based on forms it contains; explicitly teach form to support these interventions.

Both approaches take the operation of natural learning processes, using input, as essential for learning. The difference between them regards the potential for successful intervention in the processes. While (2) seeks to make learning more successful by intervening, (1) holds that it is best to simply encourage the conditions in which the natural processes will be most successful. This contrast is about the value of form focus: getting learners to pay attention to and deal with selected aspects of form.

In terms of the discussion in the previous sections, what we are talking about here is perceptual output representations and their role in learning (see Figure 2). In both approaches, when an input sentence "out there" is encountered, learners pay attention to it and become aware of it, which is to say aware of the perceptual output representation of the sentence. On the basis of this representation, phonological and syntactic representations are activated or constructed in the linguistic "place." The conceptual system seeks to derive a meaning for the sentence, based on this chain of representations and its own contextual and world knowledge. This interpretive processing necessarily interacts with the linguistic processing, helping to activate or establish linguistic representations that are appropriate for the input. The overall process may require changes in the linguistic system, simply to make sense of the perceptual output representation. This is implicit learning.

Where the two pedagogical options differ, again, is in the possibility and desirability of intervening in this process. By "intervening" here, I mean trying to lead the implicit processes to make particular changes in the linguistic system, changes they might not otherwise make.[11] Option (2) holds that we can and should do so, using what we know about grammar and about learners'

---

[11] Both options accept intervention in the sense of clarifying meaning (conceptual intervention) or of speaking clearly (auditory intervention).

needs. This intervention can take several forms, to be discussed later. Pedagogical option (1), in contrast, says we should trust the natural implicit processes to make the appropriate changes in the linguistic system, simply giving them as many opportunities as possible to do so (providing extensive input), along with any support that the conceptual processing requires (helping learners understand the input).

It is important to avoid simplistic interpretations of the pedagogical options. Authors who favor input-oriented instruction (option 1) are not calling for a ban on all mention of form in the classroom (see for example, Krashen & Terrell, 1988; Winitz, 2020). Nor are advocates of (2) simply rejecting such a ban; they are arguing that form should have a prominent role in instruction. The contrast is better seen in terms of default assumptions.

1. Form focus is *in general* not a good thing to do and so should only be used in very limited ways; identifying special cases in which it is appropriate is then a matter for research and teacher reflection.[12]
2. Form focus is *in general* a good thing to do and so should be used extensively.

In the following sections I will consider these two approaches in turn.

5.2 Trusting the Natural Processes

If input, and comprehension of input, is the heart of learning, then a natural goal for instruction is to maximize learners' exposure to the language, in ways that facilitate comprehension. This approach is thus focused on simply giving the natural processes the best opportunity to do what they do, without trying to alter what they do.

In the extreme case, trusting the natural processes can mean doing nothing more than telling learners "go read something" or "go listen to something" and leaving them on their own to carry out these instructions. While this type of assignment may have value in some contexts (I have used it as one part of class work), it is not the standard approach to input-oriented instruction. Such instruction will typically provide support, of two general types.

One type involves providing appropriate input or guiding learners in selecting their own sources. Crucially, judgments of appropriateness are not based on the particular grammatical forms or vocabulary items contained in the material but rather on comprehensibility and learners' attitude toward the materials – dealing with the input should be an interesting and pleasurable experience. The other type is help with comprehension, using aids like pictures, graphs, tables,

---

[12] See Truscott (1999, 2001) for the case of error correction.

diagrams, and realia, as well as oral or written explanations and background information. Efforts to clarify meaning can involve form in limited ways, where they are deemed useful for understanding the input and do not significantly distract learners from its meaning. Whatever form the clarification takes, its goal is to establish good conceptual representations of the input, which can then contribute to construction of appropriate linguistic (phonological and syntactic) representations – and this is the heart of second language learning.

Earlier, I briefly described the major ways that input is provided in input-oriented instruction – reading, listening, viewing, and content instruction in the target language. Considerable research has sought to test their effects and has obtained favorable overall conclusions, though in some cases these conclusions are complicated by the inclusion of various interventions, including form focus.

5.3 Trying to Assist the Natural Processes: Input-Oriented Interventions

If we accept that second language acquisition results largely from the workings of natural learning mechanisms of some sort, as most of us now do, the question remains of whether we can intervene in those natural processes to make learning more successful. Perhaps teachers can use what we know about language and about teaching techniques to push the natural processes in directions that will be most helpful for the learners, using some type of form-focused instruction. The belief that we *can* do so is now overwhelmingly favored in the SLA literature.

The term "form focus" is commonly used in this context, to mean any instruction that deliberately focuses learners' attention on formal features of the language. Such instruction appears in many varieties, only some of which are directly about input, and it is not always easy to separate the two types, in principle or in practice. In this section I will focus on those that are most clearly, explicitly tied to input. The following section will consider the question more broadly, asking if form-focused intervention in general is more effective than the alternative of simply letting the natural processes do their work through meaning-oriented input processing.

The prototypical examples of input-oriented intervention are input enhancement (Sharwood Smith, 1981) and input flood (Rutherford & Sharwood Smith, 1985; Trahey & White, 1993). These interventions are manipulations of perceptual output (see Figure 2), seeking to adjust representations at this level in ways that will alter the operations of the implicit learning processes, encouraging them to incorporate past tense endings in the interlanguage, for example. The conclusion from the research described earlier is that we do not have good reason to think that such interventions are effective.

On the theoretical side, Schmidt's noticing has been offered as a possible basis for form-focused interventions. Such efforts to draw learners' attention to a form in the input naturally encourage noticing of that form. In genuine applications of his proposal, this is best interpreted as pointing to particular aspects of the input, which can then be used by implicit processes. Schmidt was noncommittal regarding the nature of the implicit learning processes themselves, but they are perhaps most naturally associated with the implicit learning of N. Ellis (2005, 2015). The idea then is that we can assist learning by encouraging learners to notice appropriate aspects of form in their input.

The (technical) concept of noticing is actually not very helpful here, though. Schmidt's hypothesis is that learners need to notice appropriate items in the input, but apart from random examples he made no attempt to identify or characterize those items. Nor, to my knowledge, has anyone else taken up the challenge. Teachers who wish to use Schmidt's ideas are thus left with pedagogical grammars, tradition, and intuition, none of which are useful guides to how natural implicit processes work or to the underlying nature of a functioning interlanguage.

The other problem with applying the concept of noticing is that while we do not know what the targets of noticing should be, we know a lot about what they do *not* include – all the rules and generalizations that make up pedagogical grammar. Those who try to use noticing as a general guide for teaching are likely to end up abandoning Schmidt's concept (implicitly, as a general rule) and falling back on the loose notion of "awareness of something," simply because sticking to the actual meaning of the term would mean dropping most of the topics that they want to include. This describes a number of proposals that have been offered for incorporating form focus in language instruction (e.g., R. Ellis, 1993, 1995; Long & Robinson, 1998; Nassaji & Fotos, 2004). These proposals cite Schmidt's work as their foundation, but they do not in fact use Schmidt's concept of noticing and are not applications of his Noticing Hypothesis.

Altogether, research on input-oriented interventions offers little reason to think that intervening in the natural processes is beneficial. The theoretical basis for such interventions, in the form of noticing, is less than compelling, to put it mildly. Again, though, research on the effects of form-focused intervention in input processing is not easy to separate from research on form-focused intervention *in general*. So we now turn to the broader question of whether form-focused intervention is in general superior to simply relying on the natural processes.

5.4 Trying to Assist the Natural Processes: Form-Focused Intervention

There is a near-consensus among SLA researchers that it *is* in fact superior and that we can and should intervene, quite extensively. The popularity of this view is expressed well by Gass, Behney, and Plonsky (2020): "the debate over whether or not form-focused instruction is superior to input-only language teaching was largely settled [in favor of form focus] in the early-to-mid-1980s" (p. 484).[13] As a description of a social phenomenon, this is more or less accurate. But if it is taken as a claim that the research (then or now) has produced convincing support for the consensus, I suggest that skepticism is appropriate.

5.4.1 First Doubts

Do we know how language should be taught? Anyone who has been through traditional teacher training and seen the variety of methods and techniques available should be able to sympathize with a skeptical response. A bewildering variety of teaching practices is on offer (see, for example, Larsen-Freeman & Anderson, 2011), each with its own intuitive appeal and each backed by theoretical and empirical arguments and enthusiastic endorsements from learners. The different methods and approaches conflict with one another even on basic principles, to say nothing of the details of what should and should not be done in the classroom. This situation should not inspire confidence in a claim that we have resolved any fundamental issues in language teaching (or that we resolved them long ago).

A traditional, and still popular, argument for form-focused intervention is that the speech and writing of uninstructed learners is seriously flawed and therefore we need to intervene, to help them learn the right ways to say things. This of course begs the question of whether such intervention will have the desired effect. The millions of learners whose speech and writing remain riddled with grammatical errors after years of formal instruction and correction should at least raise some doubts.

5.4.2 Further Doubts: The Problem of Ignorance

To teach something, you need to have a good understanding of what you're teaching. To write a useful textbook or to train teachers, you need to have an even better understanding. For the case of language teaching, this is a tall order. The effectiveness of language instruction is inevitably limited by the fact that

---

[13] Though they do kindly note my dissenting view.

languages are insanely complex and we really don't have a good understanding of any of them. A pedagogical grammar is necessarily a superficial description, and typically bears only a passing resemblance to linguistic theories, which express our best current understanding of language – and which differ greatly among themselves, further illustrating how limited our understanding is. A teacher who has fully succeeded in the enormous task of mastering a pedagogical grammar of English, for example, will still have only a limited and superficial grasp of English grammar.

One problem with pedagogical grammar is that almost any principle we teach has many (often *very* many) exceptions. This is illustrated by an experience I have had a number of times in observing high school English classes in Taiwan. I see a particular grammar pattern explicitly taught and practiced, after which the students can successfully produce many sentences by following the rule. But a substantial portion of the sentences they come up with are not real English. They are sentences that perfectly follow the pedagogical rule but would never be used by any competent speaker of English. This instruction no doubt has value in giving low-level students some basic ability to express themselves in the foreign language, but if we are seeking something more than this – some genuine competence in the language – it is not clear if students are being helped or harmed by the instruction.

Efforts to teach language are further hampered by our limited understanding of learning processes and, partly for that reason, by our limited ability to control them. Consider first the easier (and less important) part – explicit learning. There should not be anything controversial in a statement that we have only a limited understanding of how explicit instruction of form should be carried out. The answer probably depends on the individual learner, the target of the learning, and the current circumstances, as well as the personality and abilities of the individual teacher. Truly effective teaching requires teachers to "get inside the learner's head" and work with what they find there – a very difficult task, especially when teachers have to deal with large numbers of students, as they so often do. This is not to say that explicit education is a complete waste of time – students *do* learn things. But the "easy" part is far from easy and its outcome is highly variable.

When it comes to the more important topic of *implicit* learning, we are ignorant almost by definition. To say that we are dealing with implicit knowledge and implicit learning is to say that no one is aware of what is going on when learning occurs, or fails to occur: We do not know what the underlying knowledge is supposed to look like; we do not know, at any point, what it actually does look like or just how this state compares to the desired state; we do not know how the knowledge changes in response to any given input or intervention.

This ignorance has important implications for interventions like input enhancement and input flood. When we pick out formal features or structures to highlight or to insert in the learners' input, we are treating these as real "things" in the interlanguage. We highlight "the passive" or repeatedly show learners examples of "the passive" in the hopes that they will then acquire "the passive." But it is far from clear that "the passive" is a genuine thing in the implicit grammar. It is at least as likely to be the surface manifestation of complex interactions among various abstract elements. Efforts to focus learners' attention on passive constructions might then be compared to presenting math students with complex high-level formulas when they have not yet mastered the basic background knowledge. The difference in the two cases is that for the math problem we know what the more basic knowledge should look like; for language we do not.

This does not mean the whole thing is hopeless. The possibility of developing a genuine scientific understanding, and an ability to apply it in practice, cannot be dismissed out of hand. But it does mean that skepticism is appropriate, now and for some time to come. A claim that teachers can successfully manipulate the implicit learning processes is a very strong claim.

5.4.3 And More Doubts: Ordered Development

There is considerable reason to believe that much of second language acquisition is patterned in ways that are largely independent of instruction and context and the particular languages involved (both the target language and the learner's L1). This observation is most closely associated with Krashen's (1982) Natural Order Hypothesis and Pienemann's Processability Theory (see Pienemann & Lenzing, 2020) but goes well beyond them. VanPatten, Smith, and Benati (2020) chose the term "ordered development" to describe the phenomena in general. Their existence provides another source of doubts about intervention in the natural learning processes.

First, it shows how limited the possibilities are. Altering the orders does not appear to be an option. Second, it raises large issues of feasibility. In principle, a good understanding of the phenomena could guide teaching: We determine the current stage of the learners in regard to each sequence and intervene in ways that will help them with the next stage. But the practical problems in carrying out such a plan are overwhelming. Teachers need to have a good, in-depth understanding of the sequences, an understanding that probably goes beyond what research has so far revealed. After acquiring this understanding, they need to determine where each of their students currently stands on each of the sequences, adjust their teaching accordingly, and continually retest the students to keep up with their progress through the stages. Even if these things can be accomplished, there is as yet little if any reason to think the interventions will actually have the desired effect. Not surprisingly, proposals for form-focused interventions do not typically include a program for dealing with ordered development, raising further doubts about their value.

5.4.4 The Case of Written Corrective Feedback

I have suggested that the widespread belief in the value of form focus may be more a social phenomenon than a reflection of the evidence. An illustration of this point is provided by common treatments of evidence on written error correction, now typically called "written corrective feedback," or WCF. The literature on the subject is full of statements that the research provides a good basis for advising teachers to correct their students' errors – to intervene in the natural learning processes. Particularly interesting are the favorable conclusions of various meta-analytic reviews of the research (Brown, Liu, & Norouzian, 2023; Kang & Han, 2015; Lim & Renandya, 2020; Reynolds & Kao, 2022; Russell & Spada, 2006) and the largely uncritical acceptance they have received. I have examined these meta-analyses and the research that they synthesized in some depth, concluding that there is no basis for the optimistic conclusions (see Truscott, 2007a, 2016, 2020, 2022a, 2023). A list of disturbing problems can be identified in them, some shared by all, some characterizing just some of them.

Perhaps most disturbing, though by no means most important, is the way that harmful effects were handled by Russell and Spada (2006) and Kang and Han (2015). When studies found correction harmful, yielding a negative effect size, the minus sign got lost and the effect was treated as beneficial. A more common problem is that many of the studies used in these meta-analyses did not include a no-correction group; the study just found one type of correction to be better than another – which could just as well be read "not as bad as another." These studies were inappropriately treated as evidence on whether correcting is better than not correcting.

Also included in the meta-analyses were studies that combined correction with another treatment and then invalidly attributed observed benefits to the correction. Some used tests that can tell us little or nothing about learners' ability to use what they have learned in any practical way. Others did not study learning at all but simply measured how well learners could use the corrections that were marked on their paper to correct those particular mistakes on that particular paper (with considerable success, of course, and so with large effect sizes).

Some studies that found correction ineffective or harmful were inappropriately excluded from the meta-analyses. The average effect size was inflated by the inclusion of a set of studies, all nearly identical to one another, that achieved strong results by looking only at one very simple error type, doing the treatment and testing in ways that distanced the studies both from actual language use and from actual teaching concerns, and disregarding possible harmful effects of the correction (see discussion). For most of their findings, the meta-analyses relied on results of *immediate* posttests rather than tests of longer-term effects, which are typically lower.

I don't want to suggest that these authors were being dishonest. Most of the problems were in the original studies and the reports of those studies. Other problems arise simply from the nature of meta-analysis as it is commonly practiced. The point is that the findings of these studies cannot begin to justify the positive conclusions that have been drawn from them and which appear to be almost universally accepted. It is difficult to find in the literature any recognition of the (not particularly subtle) flaws that undermine these conclusions.

The reluctance to look critically at the findings can also be seen in regard to a very significant phenomenon found in the data, for both written and oral correction (Li, 2010). If correction is beneficial, as is generally believed, then using it several times over a period of time should be greatly superior to using it only once or twice. However, the research not only fails to find such a relation but actually finds the opposite: an *inverse* correlation between the size of the effect and the extent of the treatment (duration of the study and number of times correction is given). In other words, the best results are obtained when feedback is given just a single time; in studies that provide feedback several times over a period of a few months, as is normally done in classes, the results are poor. The failure to find a positive correlation should, in itself, be cause for alarm among those in this research area. But even the presence of an inverse correlation does not seem to have set off alarm bells. Instead, it is largely ignored.

There is a widespread belief, expressed in the academic literature, that research has found written corrective feedback beneficial. But this belief has no basis in the actual research findings. If this is an illustration of how form-focus issues get settled, then the settling looks like a social/ psychological phenomenon rather than a serious assessment of the evidence.

5.4.5 The Evidence on Form-Focused Intervention

What does the evidence say about the effectiveness of form-focused interventions in general? A good starting point, again, is the statement by Gass, Behney, and Plonsky (2020) that the issue was settled in the early to mid-1980s.

VanPatten (1988), focusing on early learners, rebutted the arguments that were made in the 1980s in support of form-focused instruction. Krashen (1992, 1993) challenged the favored evidence of the time. Truscott (1998) presented an in-depth analysis of the research that had been done up to that point, concluding that it offered no support and in fact presented good reason to doubt the value of form focus. Norris and Ortega (2000), whose meta-analysis is repeatedly cited as demonstrating the value of form focus, identified a great many problems in the research and showed a cautious attitude toward the findings.

Twenty years after the supposed settling of the issue, Doughty (2003) examined the evidence for form focus and found it "tenuous at best" (p. 256). Among her major concerns was one that Norris and Ortega themselves expressed: Most of the research that had been cited as evidence simply involved the use of "explicit declarative knowledge under controlled conditions" (Norris & Ortega, p. 486). It did not test learners' ability to use their knowledge in any meaningful way. Truscott (2004), in analyzing the meta-analysis, stressed the same point and drew the overall conclusion, again, that the evidence suggested little if any practical value for form focus. The general critique of claims about form focus was updated in Truscott (2007b), in the context of a critique of the optimistic summary of the evidence presented by Nassaji and Fotos (2004). The conclusion, again, was that the evidence actually pointed to the ineffectiveness of form focus. More recent, and similarly negative discussions, can be found in Truscott (2015) and Lichtman and VanPatten (2021).

This is not the place to attempt a comprehensive or in-depth analysis of the present state of the evidence, but it is worth noting some issues that have to be taken into consideration, issues which in my judgment have not been adequately handled. The first and perhaps most important is that noted earlier: Evidence that learners can use the instructed knowledge in highly controlled artificial contexts is not evidence that they can use it in any meaningful ways. In other words, it is not evidence that the instruction was successful. The study by Terrell, Baycroft, and Perrone (1987) of the Spanish subjunctive illustrates the point. After instruction, students scored 92 percent on formal tests but showed virtually no ability to use the forms in conversation. One might hold that the instruction provided the first step and with continuing practice they would start using the forms successfully, but this would be nothing more than a statement of faith.

When instruction does yield practical ability to use the targeted forms, we also have to ask to what extent that ability will be maintained in the long term.

Many studies reporting positive effects of instruction have done no follow-up testing or have used only brief delay periods. There does not seem to be any established standard for how long the delay should be, but the one or two week periods commonly used in the research should not inspire confidence.

These are both necessary conditions for success. When instruction produces a lasting ability to perform well on formal grammar tests, this is not an indication of success; nor is a finding of meaningful benefits that disappear in a matter of weeks. This point is not consistently recognized in reviews of the evidence. It is not sufficient to point out, as has been done, that some studies find practical benefits and that some studies find lasting effects. We need to know if the lasting effects are in learners' ability to use the acquired knowledge in meaningful ways.

If a study does find genuine, durable benefits, we then have to ask if these benefits extend beyond the context of the study. Testing is typically done in the same situation in which the intervention was carried out, by the same experimenter and/or teacher, with similar or even identical tasks. These factors maximize the chances of a successful outcome. The crucial question of what will happen when they are altered has not, to my knowledge, drawn any serious research interest. A hint of what such research might find was provided by Leki (1991), in the pedagogical context. She observed that students in writing classes learned to avoid particular errors throughout the period of instruction but then returned to making those errors when writing their evaluations for the class. I suggest that this is far from an isolated case.

Another frequent limitation of the research involves insufficient attention to *overuses* of an instructed form. An example is the study by Day and Shapson (1991), which has been frequently cited as evidence that form focus is effective. Learning was defined as use of the instructed forms when the context required them; *inappropriate* uses were excluded from the analysis. High scores could thus be obtained by students who simply learned that the form exists and that the teacher wanted them to use it – even if they didn't have a clue as to how it should be used. More generally, we know that instructed learners tend to overuse a form they have been taught (see discussion), while for uninstructed learners the more common problem is underuse. Thus, whenever the analysis focuses on contexts in which the instructed form *should* be used and disregards those in which it *should not* be used, a bias is introduced in favor of positive results, making the instruction look more successful than it actually was.

This problem can occur even when the analysis explicitly includes measures of misuse. Consider the target-like use (TLU) measure.

$$\text{TLU score} = \text{correct uses} \div (\text{obligatory contexts} + \text{overuses})$$

Imagine, first, an extreme case in which learners know that they are supposed to use the instructed form but have no idea how to use it, perhaps correctly supplying it in all ten obligatory contexts and also using it in ten contexts where it does not belong. The control learners, who have not been exposed to the form, simply do not use it. The TLU measure yields a score of .5 for the instructed learners and 0 for the control group, allowing the conclusion that the instruction was highly beneficial. Even in less extreme cases, the TLU measure will often assign much greater weight to the typical problem of uninstructed learners (underuse) than to that of instructed learners (overuse), making the instruction look more successful than it was.

In such cases it might be argued that the instructed learners have taken the first step toward acquiring the form, that the overuses will gradually disappear while the correct uses remain. But such statements of belief do not constitute evidence. Alternative statements of belief would be that the learners will be stuck with the overuses indefinitely or that correct and incorrect uses will decline together or that the (flawed) declarative knowledge acquired from the instruction will hinder the development and use of the procedural knowledge that is needed for fluent and accurate use of the form. These possibilities will be considered further next.

Avoidance (Schachter, 1974) is another factor that can make instruction look more successful than it is. Learners who are confused about verb forms cannot deal with the problem by avoiding verbs – they have to use them and so have to select one form or another. But with other potentially confusing aspects of form, passives and relative clauses for example, they do have choices. Learners who feel confused about a particular structure that they have been taught might respond by trying to avoid using it. The error count is thereby reduced, wrongly pointing to successful learning. Research on form focus has not generally included a concern with this potential problem.

The common (and generally reasonable) research practice of choosing particular forms for intervention also introduces a potential bias in favor of positive results, especially on tests given immediately after the instruction or after only a short delay. Learners whose attention has recently been focused on certain forms are, for that reason alone, better prepared for a test on them. The instruction provides a good clue as to what the point of the test is – a clue which the comparison group would not have received – encouraging the instructed learners to pay special attention to the instructed forms when taking the test. Even if they are blind to the clue and have no idea what the test is actually about, the knowledge they have of those forms has been primed by the instruction. This point suggests a type of control condition which to my knowledge has never been used. If the experiment is about tense forms, as an example, the control group might simply be told at the time of the testing that they should pay special attention to tense and make a special effort to express it accurately.

A danger to be aware of when evaluating evidence, of any kind, is *confirmation bias* – the common human tendency to focus on evidence that supports your beliefs or wishes and to disregard contrary evidence. In the review by Nassaji and Fotos (2004), for example, the authors cited a large number of studies as evidence that grammar teaching is effective but made no mention of the large body of work that has pointed to the opposite conclusion. In my critique of the review (Truscott, 2007b), I noted 23 studies that had reported negative results for formal instruction and another 11 which challenged the view that error correction is beneficial. None of them were mentioned by Nassaji and Fotos. Only one appeared in their subsequent book-length treatment of the subject (Nassaji & Fotos, 2011), with no indication that its findings were problematic for their position. Other examples of this type were noted earlier, in the discussion of written corrective feedback.

A related problem is *publication bias* (see Begg, 1994). As a general rule, studies that find substantial, positive effects are more likely to be published than those with less impressive results, because journals and reviewers favor the former and because authors may decide not to submit unimpressive findings for publication. So we have to be aware of the possibility that the published literature on form focus under-represents studies that have found such interventions unhelpful.

If there is to be a serious empirical case for form-focused intervention, all of the points raised here have to be addressed in a serious manner. There seems to be only limited interest, however, in doing so, perhaps because of the widespread belief that the issue has already been settled.

5.4.6 Intervening in the Learning Process Can Be Harmful

The problems discussed to this point indicate that we should be wary of claims that form-focused intervention yields significant benefits. But this is only half the issue. Of no less importance is the question of possible *harm* resulting from such intervention. Since we do not have a good understanding of language or of learning, particularly of the unconscious processes underlying successful development, we have to recognize the possibility that harmful effects do occur: Efforts to alter natural learning for the better could actually be having the opposite effect, getting in the way of the natural processes.

The plausibility of this concern is enhanced by Ullman's (2016) observation, for learning in general, that "the learning and/or retrieval of knowledge in declarative memory may block (inhibit) the learning and/or retrieval of analogous knowledge in procedural memory" (p. 957). In second language learning, this means that (a) explicit instruction and attention to form in the input can get in the way of the natural, procedural learning; and (b) the use of explicitly learned knowledge can block the use of implicit procedural knowledge. This appears to be true for learning in general, and there is no apparent reason to expect language learning to be an exception.

One thing we know about explicit instruction is that it tends to result in *overuse* of the instructed form (e.g., Lightbown, 1983, 1985, 1987; Lightbown et al., 1980; Pica, 1983a, 1983b; Weinert, 1987). Earlier, I cited my own experience of seeing learners use pedagogical rules, in exactly the way they were taught, to produce unacceptable sentences – an experience that I believe many teachers share. The long-term outcome in such cases is not usually investigated. The hope is that the learners will eventually eliminate the incorrect uses, maybe through further instruction or corrective feedback, without also losing their ability to use the rule. But there is no apparent basis for such optimism, especially in view of Lightbown's (1983) observations (and see Weinert, 1987, for similar findings with high school learners of German as a foreign language).

Lightbown (1983) found, first, that explicit instruction of English progressive -*ing* resulted in learners greatly overusing the form, applying their declarative knowledge in contexts in which it was inappropriate. They were then explicitly taught about present singular forms, after which the frequency and accuracy of their use of -*ing* forms declined dramatically – they frequently used uninflected verb forms where progressive was required. Cross-sectional data suggested that these problems, resulting from instruction at grades 5 and 6, lingered at least into grade 10.

A related danger, which has received essentially no attention, is that teaching particular use(s) of a form will have negative effects on other uses of that form or on related forms. The findings of Ekiert and di Gennaro (2021) point in this direction, though conclusions are limited by testing and presentation issues.[14] Their study was a conceptual replication of Bitchener and Knoch's (2010) corrective feedback study, which targeted the use of English *a* and *the* for first mention and subsequent mention, respectively ("He pointed to *a* phone on the desk ... then *the* phone started to ring"). It found that corrective feedback on this function had large benefits, for this function. Ekiert and di Gennaro used the same focused feedback but then tested additional uses of *a* and *the*, finding that they were harmed by that feedback.

The positive findings of Bitchener's work, including this and two or three nearly identical experiments, carry much of the weight in favorable judgments about the value of written corrective feedback.[15] So if the observed benefits are

---

[14] See Truscott (2020); also Truscott (2023) for general discussion of Bitchener and Knoch (2010) and related research.

[15] According to the bibliometric analysis of Crosthwaite, Ningrum, and Lee (2022), Bitchener was the most cited author in this area for the periods 2001–2010 and 2011–2022.

accompanied by initially unobserved *harmful* effects, this is of great importance. The more general point is that a finding of focused benefits resulting from a particular intervention is not sufficient to show that the intervention is a good idea. The possibility of collateral damage also has to be considered.

This point extends to the use of input enhancement. Interventions are designed to make certain aspects of the input more salient, the logic being that learners will then be more likely to pay attention to those aspects and therefore more likely to acquire them. But this logic suggests an accompanying dark side. If the intervention succeeds in increasing the attention paid to one aspect of the input, this is likely to mean *de*creased attention to other aspects, including overall comprehension, with potentially harmful effects on learning. Findings of several studies suggest that such effects do occur (see Boers et al., 2017; Choi, 2017; Lee, 2007; Lee & Huang, 2008; Park, Choi, & Lee, 2012).

Researchers generally do not go out of their way to look for harmful effects, as these authors did, so there is no way to know how many other cases of apparently successful interventions have an unseen dark side. In many studies, the data analysis is almost ideally suited to hide any harmful effects that might have occurred. An example, one of many, is Day and Shapson (1991). As described earlier, the analysis excluded *inappropriate* uses. We thus have no way of knowing if the instruction induced a serious problem of overuse. The TLU measure can also hide such problems, as described earlier.

Second language learning is a slow and difficult process and is very likely to fall short of its aim. It is understandable then that teachers and researchers seek ways to make the process faster and more successful. But in doing so we need to be aware of possible problems created by these efforts. There is a traditional Chinese story in which a farmer, unhappy because his plants are growing so slowly, decides to assist the process by pulling each of them up – with predictable consequences.

5.4.7 Conclusion

In my judgment, the field of second language instruction has long been characterized by an unwarranted faith in the ability of teachers and textbook writers to influence the learning process for the better. Given all the issues noted here, it is far from clear that we can do better than to just let the natural processes do their job, through meaning-oriented input processing. And we have to take seriously the possibility that well-intended interventions are actually harming students' learning.

This is not to say that teachers are unimportant. They have prominent roles in approaches that trust the natural processes; these roles are simply different from those in traditional grammar-oriented instruction. And, of course, the subject of formal instruction is large and there is a great deal that we do not know, so we should not dismiss the possibility that form-focused intervention can be valuable. But for now at least a skeptical attitude is appropriate, particularly toward claims that the matter has been settled in favor of form focus.

5.5 Conclusion

Second language learning, if it is to have any degree of success, largely depends on automatic, unconscious processes. These processes depend on input. Input should therefore be the main focus in language instruction. The implication is that the central issue for teaching is how this focus is to be realized in practice. Two general options are available. First, we can trust the natural processes, trying to create optimal input for them and to avoid interfering in their operations. Alternatively, we can try to enhance the workings of those processes, pointing them to significant aspects of the input and/or cultivating learners' explicit knowledge of the target language in the hope that it will facilitate the implicit learning process.

The dominant view in SLA now is that the second approach is the right one; nearly everyone who writes on the subject maintains that we can and should intervene in the natural learning process. I have offered here a different perspective: For all the reasons presented in this section, skepticism is in order regarding proposals for form-focused interventions. We do not know what is likely to work, or if anything is likely to work, or if intervention will actually do more harm than good. In this context, the largely undisputed importance of input suggests that we should favor input-oriented approaches. At the very least, we need to recognize that this fundamental issue is still with us, and to adopt a serious attitude toward it.

6 What Are the Key Readings?

The amount of material that is directly about input or has important implications for the study of input is huge, and picking out a few key readings is difficult and inevitably somewhat arbitrary. But here are some good candidates, arranged by year of publication. My apologies to those who have been left out.

Corder, S. P. (1967). The significance of learner's errors. *International Review of Applied Linguistics*, 5, 161–70.

This is one of the original classics of SLA, and the source of the input-intake distinction. Corder's notion of *transitional competence* might also be considered a precursor of the *interlanguage* concept, or an alternative formulation of it.

Selinker, L. (1972). Interlanguage. *International Review of Applied Linguistics,* 10, 209–31.

This paper introduced the idea of interlanguage – a foundational idea in the study of second language learning and of input within it.

Sharwood Smith, M. (1981). Consciousness-raising and the second language learner. *Applied Linguistics*, 2, 159–68.

Sharwood Smith explored various possibilities for intervention in the learning process, including the idea of adjusting learners' input to facilitate learning.

Krashen, S. D. (1985). *The Input Hypothesis: Issues and Implications*. London: Longman.

This is Krashen's still-relevant exploration of his hypothesis that input is the essential element in second language learning.

Schmidt, R., & Frota, S. N. (1986). Developing basic conversational ability in a second language: A case study of an adult learner of Portuguese. In R. R. Day, ed., *Talking to Learn: Conversation in Second Language Acquisition*. Rowley, MA: Newbury, pp. 237–326.

The paper presents a lengthy analysis of Schmidt's efforts to acquire Brazilian Portuguese, arguing that the learning depended on his awareness that something he was encountering in the input was not yet part of his knowledge of the language – *noticing the gap*.

Gass, S. M. (1997). *Input, Interaction, and the Second Language Learner*. Mahwah, NJ: Erlbaum.

This is a classic and still influential treatment of the subject.

Schmidt, R. W. (1990). The role of consciousness in second language learning. *Applied Linguistics*, 11, 129–58.

This paper gives the original presentation of the Noticing Hypothesis and the case for it, along with worthwhile discussion of consciousness as understood in cognitive theory.

Sharwood Smith, M. (1993). Input enhancement in instructed SLA: Theoretical bases. *Studies in Second Language Acquisition*, 15, 165–79.

This paper introduced and developed the key concept of input enhancement.

Carroll, S. E. (1999). Putting "input" in its proper place. *Second Language Research*, 15, 337–88.

Carroll made a strong case that input must be understood in terms of a series of processing steps.

Krashen, S. D. (1996). The case for narrow listening. *System,* 24, 97–100.

The paper introduces the important concept of narrow listening.

Krashen, S. (2004). The case for narrow reading. *Language Magazine,* 3(5), 17–19.

The paper introduces the important concept of narrow reading.

Ellis, R. (2005). Measuring implicit and explicit knowledge of a second language: A psychometric study. *Studies in Second Language Acquisition,* 27, 141–72.

This is the author's very influential effort to establish means of distinguishing implicit and explicit knowledge in empirical research.

Truscott, J., & Sharwood Smith, M. (2011). Input, intake, and consciousness: The quest for a theoretical foundation. *Studies in Second Language Acquisition,* 33, 497–528.

In this article, closely related to Section 4 of this Element, the authors try to establish a theoretical basis for the study of awareness in learning, offering interpretations of input, intake, and noticing, all within an established cognitive framework.

Rebuschat, P. (Ed.) (2015). *Implicit and Explicit Learning of Languages.* Amsterdam: Benjamins.

This is a valuable source for ideas and research on implicit learning.

Lichtman, K., & VanPatten, B. (2021). Was Krashen right? Forty years later. *Foreign Language Annals,* 54, 283–305.

The authors offer a much-needed reassessment of the critical response to Krashen's ideas, including the importance of input and the distinction between two types of knowledge/learning.

VanPatten, B., Keating, G. D., & Wulff, S. (Eds.) (2020). *Theories in Second Language Acquisition,* 3rd ed, New York: Routledge.

This is a valuable introduction to currently prominent theories, all with implications for input, often differing. The theories are presented by their originator(s) or main proponent(s).

References

Allport, A. (1993). Attention and control: Have we been asking the wrong questions? A critical review of twenty-five years. In D. E. Meyer and S. Kornblum, eds., *Attention and Performance XIV: Synergies in Experimental Psychology, Artificial Intelligence, and Cognitive Neuroscience*. Cambridge, MA: MIT Press, pp. 182–218.

Asher, J. (2012). *Learning Another Language Through Actions*. Los Gatos, CA: Sky Oaks Productions.

Baars, B. (1988). *A Cognitive Theory of Consciousness*. New York: Cambridge University Press.

Baars, B. (1997). *In the Theater of Consciousness: The Workspace of the Mind*. New York: Oxford University Press.

Baddeley, A., Eysenck, M. W. & Anderson, M. C. (2020). *Memory*, 3rd ed., London: Routledge.

Baddeley, A., Hitch, G. & Allen, R. (2021). A multicomponent model of working memory. In R. Logie, V. Camos, and N. Cowan, eds., *Working Memory: State of the Science*. Oxford: Oxford University Press, pp. 10–43.

Beebe, L. (1985). Input: Choosing the right stuff. In S. Gass and C. Madden, eds., *Input in Second Language Acquisition*. Rowley, MA: Newbury, pp. 404–14.

Begg, C. B. (1994). Publication bias. In H. Cooper and L. Hedges, eds., *The Handbook of Research Synthesis*. New York: Russell Sage Foundation, pp. 400–9.

Behrmann, M. (2010). Agnosia: Visual. In E. B. Goldstein, ed., *Encyclopedia of Perception*. Los Angeles: Sage, pp. 32–36.

Benati, A. (2016). Input manipulation, enhancement and processing: Theoretical views and empirical research. *Studies in Second Language Learning and Teaching*, 6(1), 65–88.

Bitchener, J. & Knoch, U. (2010). The contribution of written corrective feedback to language development: A ten month investigation. *Applied Linguistics*, 31, 193–214.

Boers, F., Demecheleer, M., He, L. et al. (2017). Typographic enhancement of multiword units in second language text. *International Journal of Applied Linguistics*, 27, 448–69.

Bohn, O.-S. & Munro, M. J. (Eds.) (2007). *Language Experience in Second Language Speech Learning: In Honor of James Emil Flege*. Amsterdam: Benjamins.

Brooks, P. J. & Kempe, V. (2013). Individual differences in adult foreign language learning:the mediating effect of metalinguistic awareness. *Memory and Cognition*, 41, 281–96.

Brown, D., Liu, Q. & Norouzian, R. (2023, online). Effectiveness of written corrective feedback in developing L2 accuracy: A Bayesian meta-analysis. *Language Teaching Research*. https://doi.org/10.1177/13621688221147374.

Brysbaert, M. & Duyck, W. (2010). Is it time to leave behind the Revised Hierarchical Model of bilingual language processing after fifteen years of service? *Bilingualism: Language and Cognition*, 13, 359–71.

Carroll, S. E. (1999). Putting "input" in its proper place. *Second Language Research*, 15, 337–88.

Carroll, S. (2001). *Input and Evidence: The Raw Material of Second Language Acquisition*. Amsterdam: Benjamins.

Carruthers, P. (2006). *The Architecture of the Mind: Massive Modularity and the Flexibility of Thought*. Oxford: Clarendon.

Cenoz, J., Genesee, F. & Gorter, D. (2014). Critical analysis of CLIL: Taking stock and looking forward. *Applied Linguistics*, 35, 243–62.

Chang, A. C-S. (2019). Effects of narrow reading and listening on L2 vocabulary learning. *Studies in Second Language Acquisition*, 41, 769–94.

Cho, K. S., Ahn, K. O. & Krashen, S. D. (2005). The effects of narrow reading of authentic texts on interest and reading ability in English as a foreign language. *Reading Improvement*, 42, 58–64.

Choi, S. (2017). Processing and learning of enhanced English collocations: An eye movement study. *Language Teaching Research*, 21, 403–26.

Chun, M. M. (2000). Contextual cueing of visual attention. *Trends in Cognitive Sciences*, 4(5), 170–8.

Clahsen, H. & Felser, C. (2006). Grammatical processing in language learners. *Applied Psycholinguistics*, 27, 3–42.

Cohen, R. A. (2014). *The Neuropsychology of Attention*, 2nd ed., New York: Springer.

Collier, V. P. (1992). The Canadian bilingual immersion debate: A synthesis of research findings. *Studies in Second Language Acquisition* 14, 87–97.

Collier, V. P. & Thomas, W. P. (2017). Validating the power of bilingual schooling: Thirty-two years of large-scale, longitudinal research. *Annual Review of Applied Linguistics*, 37, 203–17.

Corder, S. P. (1967). The significance of learner's errors. *International Review of Applied Linguistics*, 5, 161–70.

Crosthwaite, P., Ningrum, S. & Lee, I. (2022 online). Research trends in L2 written corrective feedback: A bibliometric analysis of three decades of

Scopus-indexed research on L2 WCF. *Journal of Second Language Writing*, 58, 1–16. https://doi.org/10.1016/j.jslw.2022.100934.

Day, E. M. & Shapson, S. M. (1991). Integrating formal and functional approaches to language teaching in French immersion: An experimental study. *Language Learning*, 41, 25–58.

Day, R., Bassett, J., Bowler, B. et al. (2016). *Extensive Reading*. Oxford: Oxford University Press.

de Groot, A. M. B. & Starreveld, P. A. (2015). Parallel language activation in bilinguals' word production and its modulating factors: A review and computer simulations. In J. W. Schwieter, ed., *The Cambridge Handbook of Bilingual Processing*. Cambridge: Cambridge University Press, pp. 389–415.

Dehaene, S. (2020). *How We Learn: Why Brains Learn Better Than Any Machine . . . For Now*. New York: Viking.

DeKeyser, R. M. (1995). Learning second language grammar rules: An experiment with a miniature linguistic system. *Studies in Second Language Acquisition*, 17, 379–410.

DeKeyser, R. M. (2017). Knowledge and skill in ISLA. In S. Loewen and M. Sato, eds., *The Routledge Handbook of Instructed Second Language Acquisition*. New York: Routledge, pp. 15–32.

DeKeyser, R. (2020). Skill acquisition theory. In B. VanPatten, G. D. Keating, and S. Wulff, eds., *Theories in Second Language Acquisition*, 3rd ed., New York: Routledge, pp. 83–104.

D'Esposito, M. & Postle, B. R. (2015). The cognitive neuroscience of working memory. *Annual Review of Psychology*, 66, 115–42.

Doughty, C. J. (2003). Instructed SLA: Constraints, compensation, and enhancement. In C. J. Doughty and M. H. Long, eds., *The Handbook of Second Language Acquisition*. Malden, MA: Blackwell, pp. 256–310.

Dulay, H., Burt, M. & Krashen, S. (1982). *Language Two*. New York: Oxford University Press.

Ekiert, M. & di Gennaro, K. (2021). Focused written corrective feedback and linguistic target mastery: Conceptual replication of Bitchener and Knoch (2010). *Language Teaching*, 54, 71–89.

Elley, W. B. (1991). Acquiring literacy in a second language: The effects of book-based programs. *Language Learning*, 41, 375–411.

Elley, W. B. (2000). The potential of book floods for raising literacy levels. *International Review of Education*, 46, 233–55.

Ellis, N. C. (Ed.) (1994). *Implicit and Explicit Learning of Languages*. London: Academic Press.

Ellis, N. C. (2005). At the interface: Dynamic interactions of explicit and implicit language knowledge. *Studies in Second Language Acquisition*, 27, 305–52.

Ellis, N. (2015). Implicit AND explicit language learning: Their dynamic interface and complexity. In P. Rebuschat, ed., *Implicit and Explicit Learning of Languages*. Amsterdam: Benjamins, pp. 3–23.

Ellis, N. C. & Wulff, S. (2020). Usage-based approaches to L2 acquisition. In B. VanPatten, G. D. Keating, and S. Wulff, eds., *Theories in Second Language Acquisition*, 3rd ed., New York: Routledge, pp. 63–82.

Ellis, R. (1993). The structural syllabus and second language acquisition. *TESOL Quarterly*, 27, 91–113.

Ellis, R. (1995). Interpretation tasks for grammar teaching. *TESOL Quarterly*, 29, 87–105.

Ellis, R. (2005). Measuring implicit and explicit knowledge of a second language: A psychometric study. *Studies in Second Language Acquisition*, 27, 141–72.

Ellis, R., Loewen, S., Elder, C. et al. (2009). *Implicit and Explicit Knowledge in Second Language Learning, Testing and Teaching*. Bristol: Multilingual Matters.

Feddermann, M., Möller, J. & Baumert, J. (2021). Effects of CLIL on second language learning: Disentangling selection, preparation, and CLIL-effects. *Learning and Instruction*, 74, 1–12. https://doi.org/10.1016/j.learninstruc.2021.101459.

Flege, J. E. (2009). Give input a chance! In T. Piske and M. Young-Scholten, eds., *Input Matters in SLA*. Bristol: Multilingual Matters, pp. 175–190.

Fodor, J. A. (1983) *The Modularity of Mind: An Essay on Faculty Psychology*. Cambridge, MA: MIT Press.

Gascoigne, C. (2006). Explicit input enhancement: Effects on target and non-target aspects of second language acquisition. *Foreign Language Annals*, 39, 551–64.

Gass, S. (1988). Integrating research areas: A framework for second language studies. *Applied Linguistics*, 9, 198–217.

Gass, S. M. (1997). *Input, Interaction, and the Second Language Learner*. Mahwah, NJ: Erlbaum.

Gass, S. M., Behney, J. & Plonsky, L. (2020). *Second Language Acquisition: An Introductory Course*, 5th ed., New York: Routledge.

Gass, S. M. & Mackey, A. (2020). Input, interaction, and output in L2 acquisition. In B. VanPatten, G. D. Keating, and S. Wulff, eds., *Theories in Second Language Acquisition*, 3rd ed., New York: Routledge, pp. 192–222.

Gass, S. M., Spinner, P. & Behney, J. (Eds.) (2018). *Salience in Second Language Acquisition*. New York: Routledge.

Godfroid, A. (2020). *Eye Tracking in Second Language Acquisition and Bilingualism: A Research Synthesis and Methodological Guide*. New York: Routledge.

Graham, K. M., Choi, Y., Davoodi, A., Razmeh, S. & Dixon, L. Q. (2018). Language and content outcomes of CLIL and EMI: A systematic review. *LACLIL*, 11(1), 19–37.

Griffiths, T. D. (2010). Agnosia: Auditory. In E. B. Goldstein, ed., *Encyclopedia of Perception*. Los Angeles: Sage, pp. 26–8.

Hama, M. & Leow, R. P. (2010). Learning without awareness revisited: Extending Williams (2005). *Studies in Second Language Acquisition*, 32, 465–91.

Han, Z., Park, E. S. & Combs, C. (2008). Textual enhancement of input: Issues and possibilities. *Applied Linguistics*, 29, 597–618.

Hawkins, R. (2019). *How Second Languages Are Learned: An Introduction*. Cambridge: Cambridge University Press.

Henke, K. (2010). A model for memory systems based on processing modes rather than consciousness. *Nature Reviews Neuroscience*, 11, 523–32.

Iswandari, Y. A. & Paradita, L. I. (2019). Extensive reading In EFL settings: A special interview with Professor Paul Nation. *TEFLIN Journal*, 30(2), 187–96.

Ivone, F. M. & Renandya, W. A. (2019). Extensive listening and viewing in ELT. *TEFLIN Journal*, 30, 237–56.

Jackendoff, R. (1987). *Consciousness and the Computational Mind*. Cambridge, MA: MIT Press.

Jackendoff, R. (1997). *The Architecture of the Language Faculty*. Cambridge, MA: MIT Press.

Jackendoff, R. (2002). *Foundations of Language*. Oxford: Oxford University Press.

Jackendoff, R. (2012). *A User's Guide to Thought and Meaning*. Oxford: Oxford University Press.

Jeon, E. Y. & Day, R. R. (2016). The effectiveness of ER on reading proficiency: A meta-analysis. *Reading in a Foreign Language*, 28(2), 246–65.

Kang, E. Y. (2015). Promoting L2 vocabulary learning through narrow reading. *RELC Journal*, 46, 165–79.

Kang, E. & Han, Z. (2015). The efficacy of written corrective feedback in improving L2 written accuracy: A meta-analysis. *Modern Language Journal*, 99, 1–18.

Kanwisher, N., McDermott, J., & Chun, M. (1997). The fusiform face area: A module in human extrastriate cortex specialized for face perception. *Journal of Neuroscience*, 17, 4302–11.

Kennedy, S. & Trofimovich, P. (2017). Pronunciation acquisition. In S. Loewen and M. Sato, eds., *The Routledge Handbook of Instructed Second Language Acquisition*. New York: Routledge, pp. 260–79.

Koch, C. & Tsuchiya, N. (2012). Attention and consciousness: Related yet different. *Trends in Cognitive Sciences*, 16, 103–5.

Krashen, S. D. (1981). *Second Language Acquisition and Second Language Learning*. Oxford: Pergamon.

Krashen, S. D. (1982). *Principles and Practice in Second Language Acquisition*. New York: Pergamon Press.

Krashen, S. D. (1983). Newmark's 'ignorance hypothesis' and current second language acquisition theory. In S. Gass and L. Selinker, eds., *Language Transfer in Language Learning*. Rowley, MA: Newbury, pp. 135–53.

Krashen, S. D. (1985). *The Input Hypothesis: Issues and Implications*. London: Longman.

Krashen, S. D. (1992). Formal grammar instruction . . . another educator comments . . . *TESOL Quarterly*, 26, 409–11.

Krashen, S. D. (1993). The effect of formal grammar teaching: Still peripheral. *TESOL Quarterly*, 27, 722–5.

Krashen, S. D. (1996). The case for narrow listening. *System*, 24, 97–100.

Krashen, S. (2004). The case for narrow reading. *Language Magazine*, 3(5), 17–19.

Krashen, S. D. & Terrell, T. D. (1988). *The Natural Approach: Language Acquisition in the Classroom*. New York: Prentice Hall.

Kroll, J. F., Gullifer, J. W., McClain, R., Rossi, E. & Martín, M. C. (2015). Selection and control in bilingual comprehension and production. In J. W. Schwieter, ed., *The Cambridge Handbook of Bilingual Processing*. Cambridge: Cambridge University Press, pp. 485–507.

Lantolf, J. P., Poehner, M. E. & Thorne, S. L. (2020). Sociocultural theory and L2 development. In B. VanPatten, G. D. Keating, and S. Wulff, eds., *Theories in Second Language Acquisition*, 3rd ed., New York: Routledge, pp. 223–47.

Larsen-Freeman, D. (2020). Complex dynamic systems theory: The theory and its constructs. In . VanPatten, G. D. Keating, and S. Wulff, eds., *Theories in Second Language Acquisition*, 3rd ed., New York: Routledge, pp. 248–70.

Larsen-Freeman, D. & Anderson, M. (2011). *Techniques and Principles in Language Teaching*, 3rd ed., Oxford: Oxford University Press.

Lee, S.-K. (2007). Effects of textual enhancement and topic familiarity on Korean EFL students' reading comprehension and learning of passive form. *Language Learning*, 57, 87–118.

Lee, S.-K. & Huang, H.-T. (2008). Visual input enhancement and grammar learning: A meta-analytic review. *Studies in Second Language Acquisition*, 30, 307–31.

Leki, I. (1991). The preferences of ESL students for error correction in college-level writing classes. *Foreign Language Annals*, 24, 203–18.

Leow, R. P. (2015). *Explicit Learning in the L2 Classroom: A Student-Centered Approach*. New York: Routledge.

Leung, J. H. C. & Williams, J. N. (2011). The implicit learning of mappings between forms and contextually derived meanings. *Studies in Second Language Acquisition*, 33, 33–55.

Li, S. (2010). The effectiveness of corrective feedback in SLA: A meta-analysis. *Language Learning*, 60, 309–65.

Lichtman, K. & VanPatten, B. (2021). Was Krashen right? Forty years later. *Foreign Language Annals*, 54, 283–305.

Lightbown, P. M. (1983). Exploring relationships between developmental and instructional sequences in L2 acquisition. In H. W. Seliger and M. H. Long, eds., *Classroom Oriented Research in Second Language Acquisition*. Rowley, MA: Newbury House, pp. 217–43.

Lightbown, P. M. (1985). Input and acquisition for second language learners in and out of classrooms. *Applied Linguistics*, 6, 263–73.

Lightbown, P. M. (1987). Classroom language as input to second language acquisition. In C. W. Pfaff, ed., *First and Second Language Acquisition Processes*. Cambridge: Newbury, pp. 169–87.

Lightbown, P. M., Spada, N. & Wallace, R. (1980). Some effects of instruction on child and adolescent ESL learners. In R. Scarcella and S. D. Krashen, eds., *Research in Second Language Acquisition: Selected Papers of the Los Angeles Second Language Acquisition Research Forum*. Rowley, MA: Newbury House, pp. 162–72.

Lim, S. C. & Renandya, W. A. (2020). Efficacy of written corrective feedback in writing instruction: A meta-analysis. *TESL-EJ*, 24(3), 1–26.

Loewen, S. (2020). *Introduction to Instructed Second Language Acquisition*, 2nd ed., New York: Routledge.

Loewen, S. & Sato, M. (Eds.) (2017). *The Routledge Handbook of Instructed Second Language Acquisition*. New York: Routledge.

Long, M. (1983). Native speaker/non-native speaker conversation and the negotiation of comprehensible input. *Applied Linguistics*, 4, 126–41.

Long, M. H. (1991). Focus on form: A design feature in language teaching methodology. In K. de Bot, R. B. Ginsberg, and C. Kramsch, eds., *Foreign Language Research in Cross-Cultural Perspective*. Amsterdam: Benjamins, pp. 39–52.

Long, M. (1996). The role of the linguistic environment in second language acquisition. In W. Ritchie and T. Bhatia, eds., *Handbook of language acquisition: Vol. 2. Second language acquisition*. San Diego, CA: Academic Press, pp. 413–68.

Long, M. H. & Robinson, P. (1998). Focus on form: Theory, research, and practice. In C. Doughty and J. Williams, eds., *Focus on Form in Classroom Second Language Acquisition*. New York: Cambridge University Press, pp. 15–41.

MacWhinney, B. (2001). The competition model: The input, the context, and the brain. In P. Robinson, ed., *Cognition and Second Language Instruction*. Cambridge: Cambridge University Press, pp. 69–90.

MacWhinney, B. (2012). The logic of the unified model. In S. M. Gass and A. Mackey, eds., *The Routledge Handbook of Second Language Acquisition*. Abingdon/New York: Routledge, pp. 211–27.

Martínez Agudo, J. D. (2020). The impact of CLIL on English language competence in a monolingual context: A longitudinal perspective. *The Language Learning Journal*, 48(1), 36–47.

Mason, B. & Krashen, S. (2020a). The promise of "optimal input." *Turkish Online Journal of English Language Teaching*, 5(3), 146–55. http://benikomason.net/content/articles/2020-10-20-revised-the-promise-of-optimal-input.pdf.

Mason, B. & Krashen, S. (2020b). Story-Listening: A brief introduction. *CATESOL Newsletter, July*, 53(7). www.catesol.org/v_newsletters/art icle_158695931.htm.

Mason, B., Smith, K. & Krashen, S. (2020). Story-Listening in Indonesia: A replication study. *Journal of English Language Teaching*, 62(1), 3–6.

Masrai, A. (2019). Can L2 phonological vocabulary knowledge and listening comprehension be developed through extensive movie viewing? The case of Arab EFL learners. *International Journal of Listening*, 34(1), 54–69.

Mather, G. (2011). *Essentials of Sensation and Perception*. London: Routledge.

Matsuo, S. (2015). Extensive Listening inside and outside the classroom. *Kwansei Gakuin University Humanities Review*, 20, 109–15.

Mitchell, R., Myles, F. & Marsden, E. (2019). *Second Language Learning Theories*, 4th ed., New York: Routledge.

Nakanishi, T. (2014). A meta-analysis of extensive reading research. Ed.D dissertation, Temple University.

Nakanishi, T. (2015). A meta-analysis of extensive reading research. *TESOL Quarterly*, 49, 6–37.

Nassaji, H. (2017). Grammar acquisition. In S. Loewen and M. Sato, eds., *The Routledge Handbook of Instructed Second Language Acquisition*. New York: Routledge, pp. 205–23.

Nassaji, H. & Fotos, S. (2004). Current developments in research on the teaching of grammar. *Annual Review of Applied Linguistics*, 24, 126–45.

Nassaji, H. & Fotos, S. (2011). *Teaching Grammar in Second Language Classrooms: Integrating Form-Focused Instruction in Communicative Context*. New York: Routledge.

Ng, Q. R., Renandya, W. A. & Chong, M. Y. C. (2019). Extensive reading: Theory, research and implementation. *Teflin Journal*, 30(2), 171–86.

Nobre, A. C. & Mesulam, M.-M. (2014). Large-scale networks for attentional biases. In S. Kastner and A. C. Nobre, eds., *The Oxford Handbook of Attention*. Oxford: Oxford University Press. https://doi.org/10.1093/oxfordhb/9780199675111.013.035.

Norris, J. M. & Ortega, L. (2000). Effectiveness of L2 instruction: A research synthesis and quantitative meta-analysis. *Language Learning*, 50, 417–528.

O'Grady, W. (2005). *Syntactic Carpentry: An Emergentist Approach to Syntax*. Mahway, NJ: Erlbaum.

O'Grady, W. (2015). Processing determinism. *Language Learning*, 65, 6–32.

Paradis, M. (2004). *A Neurolinguistic Theory of Bilingualism*. Amsterdam: Benjamins.

Paradis, M. (2009). *Declarative and Procedural Determinants of Second Languages*. Amsterdam: Benjamins.

Park, H., Choi, S. & Lee, M. (2012). Visual input enhancement, attention, grammar learning, and reading comprehension: An eye movement study. *English Teaching*, 67, 241–65.

Pellicer-Sánchez, A. & Boers, F. (2019). Pedagogical approaches to the teaching and learning of formulaic language. In A. Siyanova-Chanturia and A. Pellicer-Sánchez, eds., *Understanding Formulaic Language: A Second Language Acquisition Perspective*. New York: Routledge, pp. 153–73.

Pica, T. (1983a). Adult acquisition of English as a second language under different conditions of exposure. *Language Learning*, 33, 465–97.

Pica, T. (1983b). Methods of morpheme quantification: Their effect on the interpretation of second language data. *Studies in Second Language Acquisition*, 6, 69–78.

Pienemann, M. & Lenzing, A. (2020). Processability theory. In B. VanPatten, G. D. Keating, and S. Wulff, eds., *Theories in Second Language Acquisition*, 3rd ed., New York: Routledge, pp. 162–90.

Piske, T. & Young-Scholten, M. (Eds.) (2009). *Input Matters in SLA*. Bristol: Multilingual Matters.

Posner, M. I. (2012). *Attention in a Social World*. Oxford University Press.

Posner, M. I. & Petersen, S. E. (1990). The attention system of the human brain. *Annual Review of Neuroscience*, 13, 25–42.

Posner, M. I. & Rothbart, M. K. (1992). Attentional mechanisms and conscious experience. In A. D. Milner and M. D. Rugg, eds., *The Neuropsychology of Consciousness*. London: Academic Press, pp. 91–111.

Rankin, T. & Unsworth, S. (2016). Beyond poverty: Engaging with input in generative SLA. *Second Language Research*, 32, 563–72.

Reber, A. S. (1993). *Implicit Learning and Tacit Knowledge: An Essay on the Cognitive Unconscious*. Oxford: Oxford University Press.

Reber, A. S. & Allen, R. (Eds.) (2022). *The Cognitive Unconscious: The First Half Century*. New York: Oxford University Press.

Rebuschat, P. (Ed.) (2015). *Implicit and Explicit Learning of Languages*. Amsterdam: Benjamins.

Rebuschat, P. (2022). Implicit learning and language acquisition: Three approaches, one phenomenon. In A. S. Reber and R. Allen, eds., *The Cognitive Unconscious: The First Half Century*. New York: Oxford University Press pp. 115–38.

Reynolds, B. L. & Kao, C.-W. (2022). A research synthesis of unfocused feedback studies in the L2 writing classroom: Implications for future research. *Journal of Language and Education*, 8(4), 5–13.

Robinson, P. (1995). Attention, memory, and the "noticing" hypothesis. *Language Learning*, 45, 283–331.

Rodgers, M. (2016). Extensive listening and viewing: The benefits of audiobooks and television. *The European Journal of Applied Linguistics and TEFL*, 5(2), 43–57.

Rodgers, M., & Webb, S. (2011). Narrow viewing: The vocabulary in related television programs. *TESOL Quarterly*, 45, 689–717.

Rogers, J., Révész, A. & Rebuschat, P. (2016). Implicit and explicit knowledge of inflectional morphology. *Applied Psycholinguistics*, 37, 781–812.

Russell, J. & Spada, N. (2006). The effectiveness of corrective feedback for the acquisition of L2 grammar: A meta-analysis of the research. In J. M. Norris and L. Ortega, eds., *Synthesizing Research on Language Learning and Teaching*. Amsterdam: Benjamins, pp. 133–64.

Rutherford, W. E. & Sharwood Smith, M. (1985). Consciousness-raising and Universal Grammar. *Applied Linguistics*, 6, 274–82.

Sanz, C. & Leow, R. (Eds.) (2011). *Implicit and Explicit Language Learning: Conditions, Processes, and Knowledge in SLA and Bilingualism.* Washington, DC: Georgetown University Press.

Schachter, J. (1974). An error in error analysis. *Language Learning*, 24, 205–14.

Schendan, H., Searl, M., Melrose, R. & Stern, C. (2003). An fMRI study of the role of the medial temporal lobe in implicit and explicit sequence learning. *Neuron*, 37(6), 1013–25.

Schmidt, R. W. (1990). The role of consciousness in second language learning. *Applied Linguistics*, 11, 129–58.

Schmidt, R. W. (1995). Consciousness and foreign language learning: A tutorial on the role of attention and awareness in learning. In R. Schmidt, ed., *Attention and Awareness in Foreign Language Learning*. Honolulu, HI: Second Language Teaching and Curriculum Center, University of Hawai'i, pp. 3–63.

Schmidt, R. W. (2001). Attention. In P. Robinson, ed., *Cognition and Second Language Instruction*. Cambridge: Cambridge University Press, pp. 3–32.

Schmidt, R. & Frota, S. N. (1986). Developing basic conversational ability in a second language: A case study of an adult learner of Portuguese. In R. R. Day, ed., *Talking to Learn: Conversation in Second Language Acquisition*. Rowley, MA: Newbury, pp. 237–326.

Schwartz, A. (2015). Bilingual lexical access during written sentence comprehension. In J. W. Schwieter, ed., *The Cambridge Handbook of Bilingual Processing*. Cambridge: Cambridge University Press, pp. 327–48.

Selinker, L. (1972). Interlanguage. *International Review of Applied Linguistics*, 10, 209–31.

Sharwood Smith, M. (1981). Consciousness-raising and the second language learner. *Applied Linguistics*, 2, 159–68.

Sharwood Smith, M. (1991). Speaking to many minds: On the relevance of different types of language information for the L2 learner. *Second Language Research*, 7, 118–32.

Sharwood Smith, M. (1993). Input enhancement in instructed SLA: Theoretical bases. *Studies in Second Language Acquisition*, 15, 165–79.

Sharwood Smith, M. (1996). *The Garden of Eden and Beyond: On Second Language Processing*. CLCS Occasional Paper no. 44, Trinity College, Dublin.

Sharwood Smith, M. (2021). Internal context, language acquisition and multilingualism. *Second Language Research*, 37, 161–70.

Sharwood Smith, M. & Truscott, J. (2014a). Explaining input enhancement: A MOGUL perspective. *IRAL*, 52, 253–81.

Sharwood Smith, M. & Truscott, J. (2014b). *The Multilingual Mind: A Modular Processing Perspective*. Cambridge: Cambridge University Press.

Slabakova, R., Leal, T., Dudley, A. & Stack, M. (2020). *Generative Second Language Acquisition*. Cambridge: Cambridge University Press.

Snow, M. A., Met, M. & Genesee, F. (1989). A conceptual framework for the integration of language and content in second/foreign language instruction. *TESOL Quarterly*, 23, 201–17.

Squire, K. & Wixted, J. T. (2011). The cognitive neuroscience of human memory since H.M. *Annual Review of Neuroscience*, 34, 259–88.

Suzuki, Y. & DeKeyser, R. (2017). The interface of explicit and implicit knowledge in second language: Insights from individual differences in cognitive aptitudes. *Language Learning*, 67, 747–90.

Swain, M. (1985). On communicative competence: Some roles of comprehensible input and comprehensible output in its development. In S. M. Gass and C. G. Madden, eds., *Input in Second Language Acquisition*. Rowley, MA: Newbury, pp. 235–53.

Swain, M. (1991). French immersion and its offshoots: Getting two for one. In B. F. Freed, ed., *Foreign Language Acquisition Research and the Classroom*. Lexington, MA: D. C. Heath, pp. 91–103.

Swain, M. (2005). The Output Hypothesis: Theory and Research. In E. Hinkel, ed., *Handbook of Research in Second Language Learning and Teaching*. Mahwah, NJ: Lawrence Erlbaum, pp. 471–83.

Tarone, E. (2014). Enduring questions from the Interlanguage Hypothesis. In Z. Han and E. Tarone, eds., *Interlanguage Forty Years Later*. Amsterdam: Benjamins, pp. 7–26.

Terrell, T. D. (1991). The role of grammar instruction in a communicative approach. *Modern Language Journal*, 75, 52–63.

Terrell, T. D., Baycroft, B. & Perrone, C. (1987). The subjunctive in Spanish interlanguage: Accuracy and comprehensibility. In B. VanPatten, T. R. Dvorak, and J. F. Lee, eds., *Foreign Language Learning: A Research Perspective*. Cambridge, MA: Newbury, pp. 119–32.

Tomlin, R. S. & Villa, V. (1994). Attention in cognitive science and second language acquisition. *Studies in Second Language Acquisition*, 16, 183–203.

Trahey, M. & White, L. (1993). Positive evidence and preemption in the second language classroom. *Studies in Second Language Acquisition*, 15, 181–204.

Truscott, J. (1998). Noticing in second language acquisition: A critical review. *Second Language Research*, 14, 103–35.

Truscott, J. (1999). The case for "The case against grammar correction in L2 writing classes": A response to Ferris. *Journal of Second Language Writing*, 8, 111–22.

Truscott, J. (2001). Selecting errors for selective error correction. *Concentric: Studies in English Literature and Linguistics*, 27, 225–40.

Truscott, J. (2004). The effectiveness of grammar instruction: Analysis of a meta-analysis. *English Teaching & Learning*, 28(3), 17–29.

Truscott, J. (2007a). The effect of error correction on learners' ability to write accurately. *Journal of Second Language Writing*, 16, 255–72.

Truscott, J. (2007b). Grammar teaching and the evidence: A response to Nassaji and Fotos (2004). *International Journal of Foreign Language Teaching.* Available on ResearchGate.

Truscott, J. (2015). *Consciousness and Second Language Learning.* Bristol: Multilingual Matters.

Truscott, J. (2016). The effectiveness of error correction: Why do meta-analytic reviews produce such different answers? In Y.-N. Leung, ed., *Epoch Making in English Teaching and Learning: Evolution, Innovation, Revolution.* Taipei: Crane, pp. 126–41.

Truscott, J. (2020). The efficacy of written corrective feedback: A critique of a meta-analysis. Unpublished manuscript. National Tsing Hua University. Available on Research Gate.

Truscott, J. (2022a). Efficacy of written corrective feedback in writing instruction: A critique of another meta-analysis. Unpublished manuscript. National Tsing Hua University. Available on Research Gate.

Truscott, J. (2022b). *Working Memory and Language in the Modular Mind.* London: Routledge.

Truscott, J. (2023). What about validity? Thoughts on the state of research on written corrective feedback. *Feedback in Second Language*, 1, 33–53.

Truscott, J. & Sharwood Smith, M. (2004). Acquisition by processing: A modular approach to language development. *Bilingualism: Language and Cognition*, 7, 1–20.

Truscott, J. & Sharwood Smith, M. (2011). Input, intake, and consciousness: The quest for a theoretical foundation. *Studies in Second Language Acquisition*, 33, 497–528.

Truscott, J. & Sharwood Smith, M. (2019). *The Internal Context of Bilingual Processing.* Amsterdam: Benjamins.

Tsang, A. (2022). Effects of narrow listening on ESL learners' pronunciation and fluency: An "MP3 flood" programme turning mundane homework into an engaging hobby. *Language Teaching Research*, 26, 434–54.

Tulving, E. (2000). Concepts of memory. In E. Tulving and I. M. Craik, eds., *The Oxford Handbook of Memory.* Oxford: Oxford University Press, pp. 33–43.

Ullman, M. T. (2016). The Declarative/Procedural Model: A neurobiological model of language learning, knowledge, and use. In G. Hickok and S. L. Small, eds., *Neurobiology of Language*. Amsterdam: Elsevier, pp. 953–68.

Ullman, M. T. (2020). The Declarative/Procedural Model: A neurobiologically motivated model of first and second language learning, knowledge, and use. In B. VanPatten, G. D. Keating, and S. Wulff, eds., *Theories in Second Language Acquisition*, 3rd edn, New York: Routledge, pp. 128–60.

VanPatten, B. (1988). How juries get hung: Problems with the evidence for a focus on form in teaching. *Language Learning*, 38, 243–60.

VanPatten, B. (1994). Evaluating the role of consciousness in second language acquisition: Terms, linguistic features & research methodology. *AILA Review*, 11, 27–36.

VanPatten, B. (2009). Processing matters in input enhancement. In T. Piske and M. Young-Scholten, eds., *Input Matters in SLA*. Clevedon: Multilingual Matters, pp. 47–61.

VanPatten, B. (2015). Foundations of processing instruction. *International Review of Applied Linguistics*, 53, 91–109.

VanPatten, B. (2017). Processing instruction. In S. Loewen and M. Sato, eds., *The Routledge Handbook of Instructed Second Language Acquisition* (pp. 166–80). New York: Routledge.

VanPatten, B. (2020). Input processing in adult L2 acquisition. In B. VanPatten, G. D. Keating, and S. Wulff, eds., *Theories in Second Language Acquisition*, 3rd ed., New York: Routledge, pp. 105–27.

VanPatten, B., Keating, G. D. & Wulff, S. (Eds.) (2020). *Theories in Second Language Acquisition*, 3rd ed, New York: Routledge.

VanPatten, B., Smith, M. & Benati, A. G. (2020). *Key Questions in Second Language Acquisition: An Introduction*. Cambridge: Cambridge University Press.

Watzinger-Tharp, J., Rubio, F. & Tharp, D. S. (2018). Linguistic performance of dual language immersion students. *Foreign Language Annals*, 51, 575–95.

Webb, S. (2015). Extensive viewing: Language learning through watching television. In D. Nunan and J. C. Richards, eds., *Language Learning Beyond the Classroom*. New York: Routledge, pp. 159–68.

Weinert, R. (1987). Processes in classroom second language development: The acquisition of negation in German. In R. Ellis, ed., *Second Language Acquisition in Context*. Englewood Cliffs, NJ: Prentice-Hall, pp. 83–99.

White, E. J., Titone, D., Genesee, F. & Steinhauer, K. (2017). Phonological processing in late second language learners: The effects of proficiency and task. *Bilingualism: Language and Cognition*, 20(1), 162–83.

White, L. (2020). Linguistic theory, Universal Grammar, and second language acquisition. In B. VanPatten, G. D. Keating, and S. Wulff, eds., *Theories in Second Language Acquisition*, 3rd ed., New York: Routledge, pp. 19–39.

Williams, J. N. (2005). Learning without awareness. *Studies in Second Language Acquisition*,27, 269–304.

Winitz, H. (Ed.) (1981). *The Comprehension Approach to Foreign Language Instruction*. Rowley, MA: Newbury.

Winitz, H. (2020). *Comprehension Strategies in the Acquiring of a Second Language*. Cham, Switzerland: Palgrave Macmillan.

Wolfe, J. M., Kluender, K. R., Levi, D. M. et al. (2018). *Sensation and Perception*, 5th ed., New York: Oxford University Press.

Young-Scholten, M. (1994). On positive evidence and ultimate attainment in L2 phonology. *Second Language Research*, 10, 193–214.

Cambridge Elements

Second Language Acquisition

Alessandro G. Benati
University College Dublin

Alessandro G. Benati is Professor and Head of the School of Education at University College Dublin. He is visiting and honorary professor at the University of York St. John, Anaheim, and the University of Hong Kong. Alessandro is known for his work in second language acquisition and second language teaching. He has published ground-breaking research on the pedagogical framework called Processing Instruction.

John W. Schwieter
Wilfrid Laurier University, Ontario

John W. Schwieter is Associate Professor of Spanish and Linguistics, and Faculty of Arts Teaching Scholar, at Wilfrid Laurier University. His research interests include psycholinguistic and neurolinguistic approaches to multilingualism and language acquisition; second language teaching and learning; translation and cognition; and language, culture, and society.

About the Series

Second Language Acquisition showcases a high-quality set of updatable, concise works that address how learners come to internalize the linguistic system of another language and how they make use of that linguistic system. Contributions reflect the interdisciplinary nature of the field, drawing on theories, hypotheses, and frameworks from education, linguistics, psychology, and neurology, among other disciplines. Each Element in this series addresses several important questions: What are the key concepts?; What are the main branches of research?; What are the implications for SLA?; What are the implications for pedagogy?; What are the new avenues for research?; and What are the key readings?

Cambridge Elements ≡

Second Language Acquisition

Printed in the United States
by Baker & Taylor Publisher Services